Sacred Complex

of

Ujjain

RECONSTRUCTING INDIAN HISTORY & CULTURE

(ISSN 0971-3824)

1. Society in Ancient India by Sures Chandra Banerji (ISBN 81-246-0000-7)
2. Political Thought in Ancient India by G.P. Singh (ISBN 81-246-0001-5)
3. Early Indian Historical Tradition and Archaeology by G.P. Singh (ISBN 81-246-0005-8)
4. Vasantotsava : The Spring Festivals of India by Leona M. Anderson (ISBN 81-246-0011-2)
5. Ecological Readings in the Veda by M. Vannucci (ISBN 81-246-0009-0)
6. Vṛndāvana in Vaiṣṇava Literature by Maura Corcoran (ISBN 81-246-0024-4)
7. Social History of the Tamils (1707-1947) by P. Subramanian (ISBN 81-246-0045-7)
8 Ancient Indian Coinage by Rekha Jain (ISBN 81-246-0051-1)
9. Buddhism and Socio-Economic Life of Eastern India by Bimal Chandra Mohapatra (ISBN 81-246-0055-4)
10. Candragupta Maurya by P.L. Bhargava (ISBN 81-246-0056-2)
11. Mṛtyu: Concept of Death in Indian Traditions by Gian Giuseppe Filippi (ISBN 81-246-0072-4)
12. Yama : The Glorious Lord of the Other World by Kusum P. Merh (ISBN 81-246-0066-X)

Reconstructing Indian History and Culture, no. 13

Sacred Complex of Ujjain

D.K. Samanta

Foreword by
Baidyanath Saraswati

D.K. Printworld (P) Ltd.
NEW DELHI-110015

Cataloging in Publication Data — DK

Samanta, Dipak Kumar, 1946-
Sacred complex of Ujjain.
(Reconstructing Indian history and culture; no. 13).
Includes bibliographical references (p.).
Includes Index.

1. Siva (Hindu deity) — Cult. 2. Hindu cults — India — Ujjain. 3. Temples, Hindu — India — Ujjain. 4. Hindu pilgrims and pilgrimages — India — Ujjain. 5. Ujjain, India — Religious life and customs. 6. Sacred place — India — Ujjain. I. Title. II. Series (Reconstructing Indian history and culture; no. 13).

ISBN 81-246-0078-3
First Published in India in 1997

Published by :
D.K. Printworld (P) Ltd.
Regd. office : '*Sri Kunj*', F-52, Bali Nagar
New Delhi - 110015
Phones: (011) 545-3975, 546-6019; *Fax*: (011) 546-5926

Printed at: DP's Impressive Impressions, New Delhi- 110059

Foreword

THE Western tradition of sociology holds that every religious conception of the universe implies a distinction between the "sacred" and the "secular", the two mutually exclusive and contradictory categories. This theory runs through the main currents of sociology of religion in India. What it brings home is a semantic system containing the various binary oppositions between the sacred and the profane, the pure and the impure, the auspicious and the inauspicious, the good sacred and the bad sacred, the auspicious sacred and the inauspicious sacred, and the various symbolic codes of hot and cold, up and down, right and left, living and dead, cardinal points in space, sound and silence, and so on and so forth. Contrary to this theory is the Indian vision of *advaita* (non-dualism) which is not merely an ontological principle — a logical inference in the thought structure — but a major aspect of the social structures and cultural traditions of India.

There is another stream of thought which signifies a break from the main tradition. As against the theory of binary opposition, it epitomises the notion of continuum between the sacred and the secular. Here the basic assumption is that the sacred and the secular are dialectically rather than dichotomously related. They are the two sides of the same coin; their difference lies in the perception of the observer, depending on what angle one looks at.

These categories are closely connected with the concepts of space and time.

Following L.P. Vidyarthi's (1961) prodigious concept of 'sacred complex', several scholars have studied the places of pilgrimage in terms of 'sacred centre', 'sacred cluster', 'sacred segments', 'sacred zone', etc. In all such studies the sacred/secular dichotomy has been maintained with unfaltering clarity.

The Sanskr̥it word *ksetra* (Pāli *khetta*), with a particular degree of generality, refers to physical space of all types: field, landed property, enclosed spot of ground, portion of space, place of origin, dominion, region, etc. The core meaning is extended to a conglomerate of wide-ranging aspects from geometric forms to metaphysical expression: plane figures like a triangle, circuit, superficies, a house, a town, seat, sphere of activity, source, extent, wife, womb, body, primeval soul or matter. The total field of spatial meaning is transformed when used in the physical and spiritual contexts. The word *kṣetra* and its derivatives occur one-hundred-and-seventy-five times in the Vedic texts alone, with wide-ranging meaning. For the first time it finds mention in the *Ṛgveda*, most commonly to denote geographical space, land, field, region or expanse of country. The conception of sacred space found its greatest development in the *Purāṇas*. *Tīrtha kṣetra* was eulogised as a microcosm. *Kṣetra* now stands for spiritual space. All sacred places are not *kṣetra*. As a place of pilgrimage, they are *tīrthas*. Only a cluster of *tīrthas* of special spiritual significance is given the categorical term *kṣetra*. Briefly, *kṣetra* is so uniquely structured in the semantic field that it becomes central to any comprehensive view of man and space. From the *kṣetra* (space) emerges the *kṣetra* (body); from the *kṣetra* (womb) the *kṣetra* (body) grows. He who lives in *kṣetra* (body) is the *kṣetrajña* (individual soul). The *rūpakṣetra* (image panel) contains *kṣetrajña* (image of the Universal Self).

Reflected in that consciousness, space is of uneven quality; it is diverse and discontinuous. All places are not suitable for sacred performances; some are more effective in this sense than others. The effectiveness of a place depends on its association with gods, sages, ancestors, spirits, and primeval events. A place is consecrated by the power of *mantra*. Even within a sacred space there are "purity space" and "protection space", each endowed with efficient powers but functionally different from the other. Like space, time also has multiple systems. Ritual space and ritual time are inextricably bound together. The sacred-effectiveness of a ritual act increases manifold with the correct combination of space and time. Bathing in a sacred river at any time, or bathing in a river on an auspicious time, is endowed with merit. But bathing at the confluence of the three rivers — the Gaṅgā, the Yamunā and the Sarasvatī — at Prayāg during *Kārtika* (October/November) has a special merit. And bathing at Prayāg, Haridvār, Nāsik and Ujjain on the occurrence of *kumbha* (the jar of nectar which emanated during the churning of the milk of ocean) festival, marking the 12-year cycle of the primeval event, has inexhaustible merit. The *tīrtha kṣetra*, as a spiritually perceived microcosm, enshrines not only all the sacred places (*tīrthas*) on the earth but also all the suns, the moons, the stars and the planets, the seasons, and the divisions of time in their essence. All rituals and festivals are observed in ritual space-time.

All existence is time. But ritual time is different; it is rooted in non-existence. The ultimate goal of all rituals is to transcend the temporal time (*anityakāla*). Ritual time must reflect, therefore, the aspect of *nityakāla*, or Mahākāla, the Great Time. The difference between *anityakāla* and *nityakāla* is fundamental. The former is characterized by *karma* (act), *krama* (order) and *kāla* (time); the later by *akarma* (non-act), *akrama* (no-order) and *akāla* (no-time). Kāla and Mahākāla are essentially connected. Kāli, *mahāśakti* (the great energy of time), is the consort of Mahākāla. The awareness of this truth is reflected in the acceptance of the lunar time by all the "timeless" societies. It finds its finest expression in Indian art: in the visual image of the Moon (the lunar time), the Gaṅgā (the flow of time) adorning the matted hair (the spidery thread of time), and *kālavyāla* (the serpent of time) hanging round the blue neck of the Mahākāla, the Great Time — the creator of creators, the preserver of preservers, the destroyer of destroyers, the nameless, the formless, the unknowable, the one whose spiritual vibrations can be felt in Ujjain, the earthly abode of Śiva, the auspicious Lord of the Great Time.

I specially welcome this book because, unlike most other studies on the 'sacred complex' theme, it is built around a 'culture area approach' brilliantly conceived within anthropology. Appropriately, the author begins with a cultural-historical account of ancient Avantī (Mālwā) and Avantikā (Ujjainī) and, then, moves on to describe the city of Ujjain as a great centre of pilgrimage. For obvious reasons, Dr. Samanta is concerned with much else, in particular, the Lord Mahākāla whose presence in Ujjain comprises and transcends everything that exists in space and time. By re-stating and identifying the twelve *Jyotirliṅgas* that keep the Hindu world alive in India today, he explores the process of linking cultures and geographical regions on a ground of pilgrimage. Clearly the emphasis is on history and anthropology, on the interface between space and time, which is appropriate in our age. But let us not forget that the text of Indian tradition makes a broad claim about the Hindu 'sacred complex'. The Paurāṇic text extricates itself from the forms of historicism and provides a direct and fruitful knowledge of cosmogony available to a wider range of people than the small group of anthropologists and historians.

At the cosmogonic level Ujjain is associated with the origin of things (from the churning of the 'milk of ocean'), the primeval war (between gods and demons), the life eternal (drops of nectar that fell on the earth), the Great Time (Mahākāla), and the marvellous mystery of *mukti* (salvation). Cosmogony is not history, not even anthropology. But it reveals the true nature of a cultural universe that gives the 'sacred complex' a spiritual status. Ujjain has acquired a meaning, a value and a spiritual nostalgia precisely because of its cosmogonic myth from the dawn of creation. Myth is more than linear history and more than evolutionary anthropology seeking empirical reality. As *tīrtha kṣetra*, Ujjain is a symbol. A symbol is not what it symbolises, but it admits the value of faith and hope in salvation — the very essence of pilgrimage, the very core that sustains the 'sacred complex' of Ujjain. Faith is not to be confused with the 'fact' of history or of science. We can compare myth with history, history with *Purāṇa* and science with scripture only at our peril. The 'sacred complex' is a thing of 'cultural experience', not an erroneous conclusion of reason.

I am grateful to Dr. D.K. Samanta for asking me to write a Foreword to his book which is rich in materials of great interest and value, particularly, to historians and anthropologists of Indian culture.

Baidyanath Saraswati

Preface

THE study of complex societies which started in India a few decades back was a turning point in Indian Anthropology. The peasant villages and the civilization of which they are a part have drawn the attention of researchers in this field. They have highlighted the complexities of such centres and the way these operate. The question which has haunted me for years was focussed on the role these centres performed and how such centres continued to remain sacred. This and similar questions aroused my interest and led me on to conduct such a study on Ujjain.

Ujjain is one of the important Hindu sacred centres. It is a centre of pilgrimage, a venue for the *Kumbha melā*, a commercial centre and it was the capital of ancient dynasties. In Hindu tradition pilgrimage is an important aspect. There is an elaborate system through which interlinkages are maintained between pilgrimage centres. The pilgrims demand specialised services on special occasions. I have also come across certain trades associated with such centres which have a good market outside. The traditional system of education and training also exist in such centres. Besides, there is the organisation of ascetics. The role of the sacred centre in various aspects of life of the common people is also an area of interest. It is of added interest to understand the interplay of these various factors.

So when I visited Ujjain in connection with a project, "Study of Urban Centres" in which I was involved, I was impressed with the city and decided to take up a detailed study. I felt that the traditional role of Ujjain as a centre of integration required to be understood in its proper perspective. How it helped the great traditional elements to percolate to the remote villages would certainly be of interest!

These were some of the factors that acted as a driving force and persuaded me to take up the present study.

A number of persons and institutions extended their constant help at various stages of this work. Though it is not possible here to express my thanks to each and every one of them, I would nevertheless mention a few who offered a warm and helping hand. Prof. B.N. Saraswati took time from an already impossible schedule to guide and advise me. He was a *pathpradarshak* or pathfinder for me in the true sense. Also, he has been generous enough to write the foreword to this book. Dr. B.M. Singhal of Ujjain University graciously extended all possible help. Were it not for the hospitality of Dr. Singhal I might not have taken up this study. I am also grateful to Padmashri Dr. V.S. Wakankar who generously shared his knowledge of Ujjain with me. Prof. L.P. Vidyarthi made me conscious of the intricacies of a sacred centre. I have also been greatly profited from my discussions with Prof. A.K. Danda. I express my sincere gratitude to the *pujārīs*, *paṇḍās* and pandits for supplying me with valuable data. Pandit Anand Shankar Vyas was a great help in making me understand the various rites performed in Ujjain. My brother B.B. Samanta (Cap.) was a constant source of inspiration. My daughter Disharee and son Tanmay shared my anguish and extended their cooperation.

D.K. Samanta

Contents

Dedicated to

Ila, my didi (sister) and Tapati, my wife,
who remained a constant source
of encouragement.

UJJAIN & SACRED NETWORK

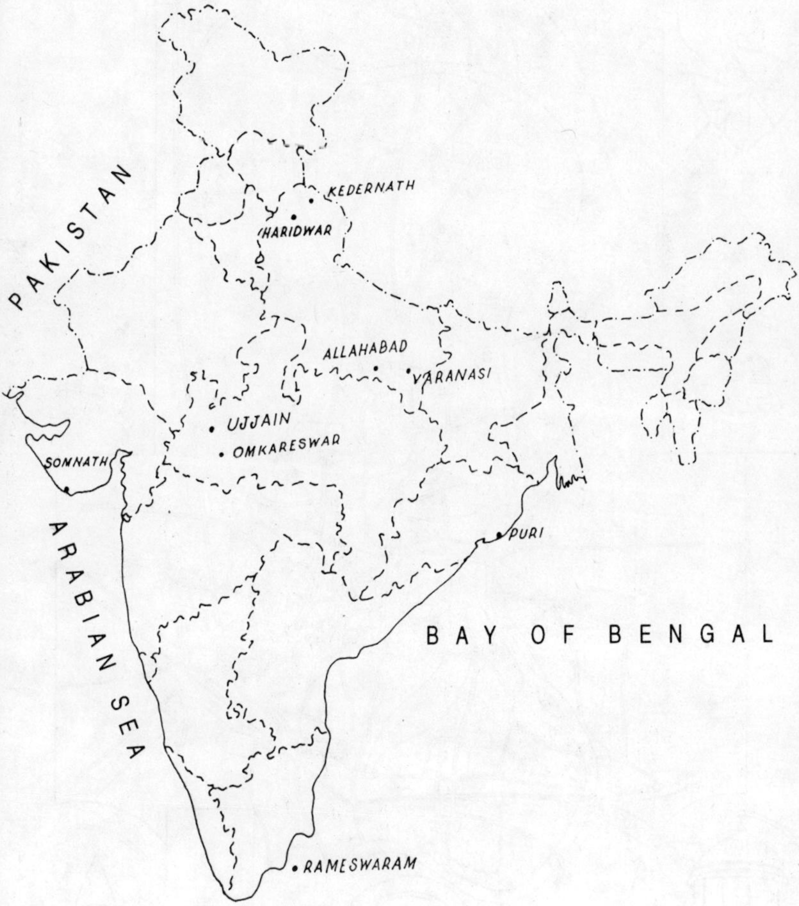

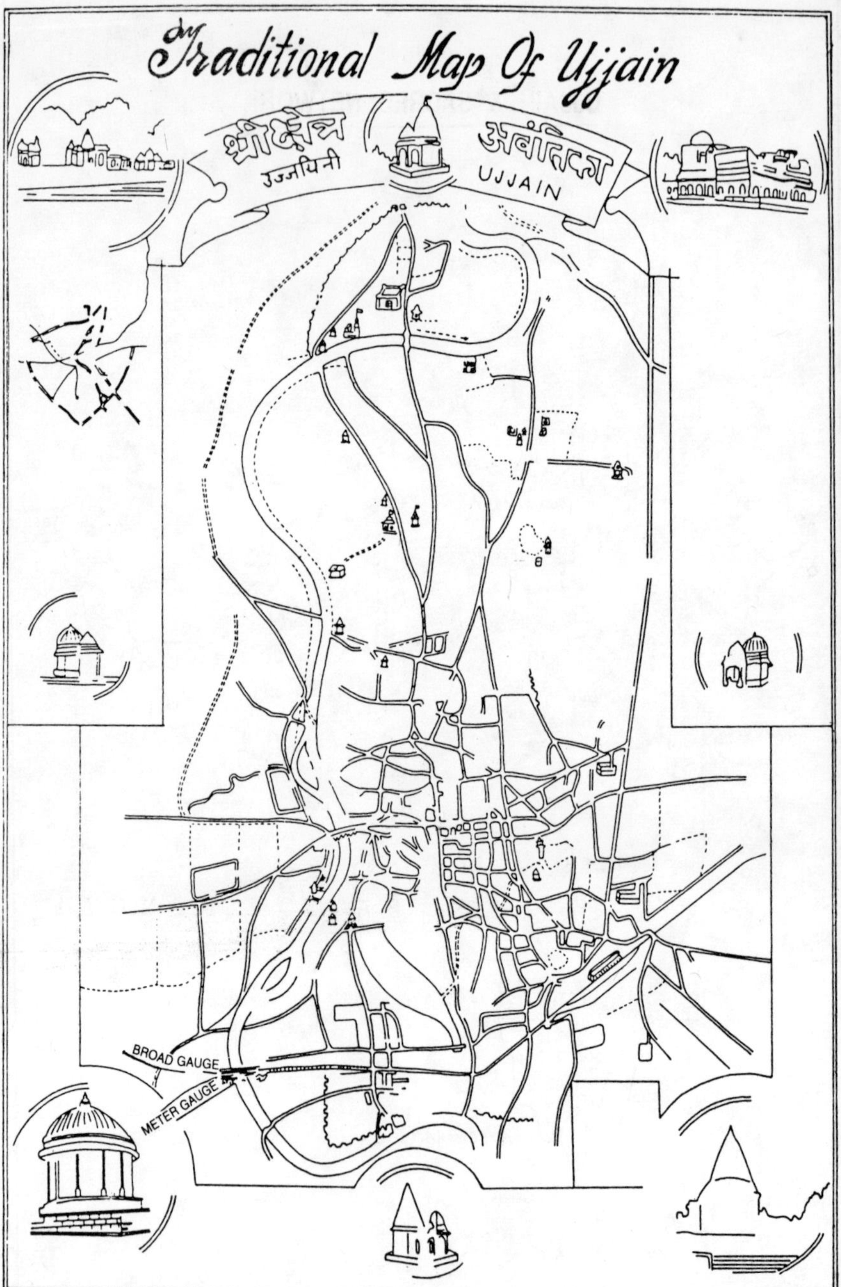
Traditional Map Of Ujjain
उज्जयिनी
अवंतिका
UJJAIN
BROAD GAUGE
METER GAUGE

1

Introduction

ANTHROPOLOGICAL research in the New World has revealed a number of culture areas. For example, the United States and Canada comprise nine culture areas. These are: the Plains, Plateau, California, the North Pacific Coast, Eskimo, Mackenzie, Eastern Woodland, South Eastern and South Western culture areas. The names used to designate these culture areas have a geographical base and to a considerable degree, they characterise the territories covered. These attempts were a follow-up of the concept developed by Clark Wisler in the early twenties. Each of these wholes embraces a large number of diverse tribal cultures which belong to one type or have some commonness, affinity and homogeneous traits so that the culture area defines the range of the culture type. Similar attempts have been made in the case of Africa (Herskovits, 1962). These culture areas were discovered due to the synthetic treatment of the data collected from America and Africa. Strangely enough, in Eurasia, there is little in the literature concerning culture areas. The civilised nations and extinct cultures have been set aside to avoid confusion. But this is more or less an escapist attitude. In these areas we may get definable culture areas. More so there are geographical wholes in these two continents.

In India, there is a need for understanding of the regional diversities in the country. There are diversities in the cultural elements of different locales. Each major linguistic region has its unique hierarchy of castes and is thus separated from adjacent regional hierarchies not only by difference of language but also by lack of marriage (Karve, 1953). It is also separated by the absence of those defined, ritualised relations of ranks which are essential to Hindu India. The areas of the principal spoken languages or dialects generally show some cultural distinctiveness and they may be called sub-regions (Mariot, 1958). Geographical dimension adds to the homogeneity of the cultural elements. There is every likelihood of the presence of a cultural type.

Traditionally in anthropology, the researcher was free to determine the limits of his study group. Often the subject of study was a small relatively homogeneous and isolated group in which cultural boundaries were coterminous with geographical, linguistic and associational boundaries. In such a case the field worker did not have to be concerned with the problem of homogeneity because he was able to choose a group, small and isolated, for observation where a high degree of homogeneity was almost certain to exist. At a complex level, when the peasant community was taken as the unit of study, its geographical boundaries still proved satisfactory in defining the limits of a cultural whole. But this kind of isolation of the peasant communities was not universally accepted. Redfield and Foster have pointed out that the peasant community in most parts of the world is not isolated from contacts with the surrounding communities and with the distant centres of urban civilisation, and it is actually dependent for many necessities of village life on the world outside. Yet for purposes of study the 'little community' is undeniably an isolable, relatively homogeneous entity. The village can usually be described adequately in terms of a common culture of shared values and world-view, shared techniques and customs.

II

The present-day interest is in the larger whole of which these communities are but a minute part. Redfield noted :

> In the case of civilised societies and nation states . . . . the problem is how to understand a community that is not only a simple band or village but is perhaps many villages in important relationship with towns and cities. Because no one village is really independent, but is a part of a much larger and more complicated system. Our interest is drawn towards the description of the more complicated system. Detaching one's self, so to speak, from the village one moves to consider the whole region or even the whole nation state as the entity to be studied and understood. (Redfield, 1955)

In the study of complex cultures, being unable to limit the cultural unit by the previous considerations of size, isolation and homogeneity, the researcher has to consider societal boundaries drawn by political accidents and traditions coupled with geographical demarcations for the selection of the area of study. Through this we can find a common core of culture in the behaviour and beliefs of a large and diverse group of people. This will be useful for understanding of the regional cultures of a nation state.

III

The urban centres in India even in the early ages were linked with the rural areas around. Every centre has a command area. There are overlappings of influences. In general, these centres should be seen as formed and functioning in relationship to extensive networks and against same background of cultural diversity. The area specialisation of these centres is not clearly demarcated. These cities are of several kinds — some are administrative centres, some are centres of pilgrimage, etc. The area served by a centre may differ along with the nature of functions. At the sacred centres, the specialists gather. Centres in the network of pilgrimages naturally display many orders of shrines, priests, teachers and religious experts of all sorts. (Redfield and Singer, 1954; Vidyarthi, 1958). Again, religious networks witness periodic pilgrimages as well as the constant movement of professionals, religious entertainers, preceptors and holy men. (Ghurya, 1953) Such religious networks have always been vital channels of cultural communication. These centres are the microcosmic centres. The pilgrims, in course of their pilgrimage, become aware of Indian civilisation as multiple layers of diversity. These centres, as said earlier, overlap in jurisdiction. But they provide the core to a culture area.

An interesting distinction is made by Redfield and Singer (1954) between two types of civilisation—the primary civilisation or the result of orthogenetic growth, developed from an indigenous folk culture and the secondary civilisation, the product of foreign cultural influence impinging on native forms. India and China have been cited as a good example of the former type. But India was not an isolated area. It had trade ties with the Middle East, Far East and South-East Asian countries, even in ancient and proto-historic periods. Besides, from the north-western front, hordes of invaders have come time and again. The country had sub-regions. The invaders settled in different parts. Though they mainly concentrated at the administrative centres or political capitals, yet their influences reached the villages too. These groups carried with them their own cultural elements. Local tradition and the foreign influences were in constant interaction to shape the regional culture.

In India the culture areas are not in the form of watertight compartments. Culture areas identified on the basis of specific cultural items constitute more or less an interlocking chain that delineates the border area (Danda, 1981). Such zones exist in spite of various attempts of integration in various periods (Ādi Śaṅkara to the present nation state). These sub-regions have to be studied for a proper understanding of the national culture.

Their diversities have to be considered. Attempts for such studies are very rare on an area basis. The tradition of area study started in the early seventies (Chhattisgarh Area Study — Danda). But this was not done in other sub-regions. Moreover, in this study, the major emphasis was given on the tribal population of the core area. The major interest was not in an interactional pattern, but rather in studying individual tribal groups. Multicaste village studies were marginally done and it was mainly tribe *vis-a-vis* caste studies. The various aspects of social life were not studied uniformly. The ethnic group was the unit of study and not a particular phenomena. The study is of high intellectual quality otherwise. A group of good ethnographic studies of classical pattern was brought in with extreme care and caution.

IV

The homogeneity can be better studied by concentrating on a single aspect of culture. This is not to deny the interlinks with other aspects; rather it is a matter of emphasis and for the purpose of limiting the workload. The belief system stands for the forces of change and external influence to a considerable degree. As an aspect of study, this may best serve our present endeavour. At the sub-regional level, the study of a pilgrim centre and its implication to the system of ritual, festival and belief in the rural areas seems imperative as a pre-condition for understanding the commonness. And such studies did not attract the attention of the anthropologist working in India.

Keeping these things in view, the present attempt has been made to study the various aspects of a pilgrim centre and to find its links with a group of multi-ethnic villages around. The centre is located in a traditional sub-zone. We have selected this sub-zone considering a few important factors. The area goes by the name of Mālwā, the western part of Madhya Pradesh State. In studying the religious life in Mālwā, Hindus being the major group, people of other faiths have not been studied.

V

The area is Mālwā, the pilgrim centre is Ujjain and the villages are within a radius of fifty kilometres. At Ujjain the ruling deity is Lord Mahākāl who is one form of Lord Śiva. It is one of the twelve self-effulgent (*Jyotirliṅga*) *liṅga*s in the country. We have studied the Mahākāl cult as a module for understanding the interplay of the sacred and the secular.

In India attempts towards integration were made in different periods. Through worship this was very prominent in all the three different philosophies — *Śaiva, Vaiṣṇava* and *Śākta*. There are twelve *Jyotirliṅga*s, fifty-two *pīṭha*s and a number of *Vaiṣṇava* pilgrim centres in the subcontinent. Ādi Śaṅkarācārya tried to unify the followers of various saints and philosophies and established four Śaṅkaramaṭhas in the country. A rough area distribution also existed which was never strictly observed. There are four *dhāmas* and visiting these means performance of a pilgrimage. The *dhāmas* are in the four directions. This does not however interfere with the formation of sub-zones. And Mālwā is no exception.

The first advantage in favouring Ujjain for study is its location. Āryāvartta of the olden days comprises the land between the Himālayas and the Vindhyan ranges. Actually the Vindhyas separate the country into two sections, Āryāvartta and Dakṣiṇātya or Deccan. Mālwā is at the junction of these two, with the maximum portion belonging to the former. This traditional division has its bearing on the cultural elements of these areas. They differ in language too. Mālwā is again at the centre of the subcontinent. From historical, political and administrative points of view, Mālwā has enjoyed a distinct identity for long. Attracted by the fertile land of the region, waves of invaders and ethnic groups have settled down in the area. It has a diverse population including tribal, peasant, and urban communities. They live in different stages of economy, from settled agriculture to the highly industrialised group in urban centres. They have a common dialect, Mālwī. The mother stock is Śaurasenī Prākṛt and it has actually come from Avantya Apabhraṁśa. Mālwā was the Avanti of the olden days and Avantikā or Ujjain enjoyed the status of capital of this *janpad* since ancient times. These are some of the important considerations for selecting Ujjain for the present study. The locational factor was the most important one since the ancient days. It was also the gateway for the Deccan and Āryāvartta.

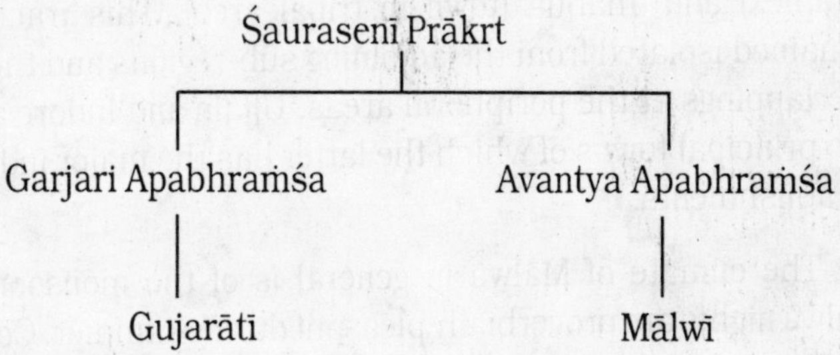

Mālwā is the tableland forming the western part of Madhya Pradesh. It is a plateau with an average elevation of 1500 feet from mean sea level stretching some 200 miles from north to south and one hundred and fifty miles from east to west. The Vindhya mountains and the river Narmadā form its southern boundary, while the river Chambal and Arāvallī hills lie on the west. On the north the plains of Bundelkhaṇḍ and the Ganges Valley form the boundary. The transition is less marked on the east. However, the river Betwā is considered as the eastern limit of the zone. For the most part the tableland consists of a great plain of black, fertile soil. This stretch is intersected by low hills and shallow valleys. During the summer, the land gives a rugged look while after the first rain, the green mantle of grass looks gorgeous. The region can be broadly divided into two — Deccan Lava formation area and to its south, the Vindhyan scrapland. The former part (northern section) is a fertile land. The Chambal river system or the upper Chambal river system drains out the rain water. River Chambal with its tributaries, including the river Śiprā, flows north to meet Yamunā. The slope is from south to north. Yamunā meets the holy Ganges near Allāhābād. So the water from the plateau drains into the Ganges.

Mālwā consists of the districts of Ujjain, Dhār, Dewās, Indore, Ratlām, Mandsaur and parts of Nimar (north of Narmadā). The first five districts form the core of the region. Ujjain is the cultural centre of Mālwā. There are five main urban centres in Mālwā — Ujjain (religious, historical and cultural centre), Mandsaur and Dhār (historical), Indore (modern industrial complex) and Jhābuā (town in tribal area). This tract never remained isolated from the adjoining sub-regions and there are overlappings at the peripheral areas. Ujjain and Indore are the two principal towns of which the latter has the major industrial establishments.

The climate of Mālwā in general is of the monsoon type. Mālwā nights are proverbially pleasant during summer. Common parlance says, "the dawn of Banāras, the evening of Ayodhyā and the night of Mālwā" stand for climatic comforts and natural beauty *par excellence*. All the three seasons, the summer, the rainy season and the winter, are distinct. From *cait* to *jeṭh* is the summer (April to June). The average temperature is eighty degrees Fahrenheit and sometimes, it shoots up to one hundred degrees. Rains start from *āṣāḍha* and last up to the middle of *kuār* (July to October). Middle of *kuār* to *phagūn* (November to March) are the winter months. The soils may be divided into three categories according to the rate of yield — *kāli māṭī* (black cotton soil), *bhūrī māṭī* (brown soil), *bhātorī māṭī* (rocky soil). All the soil types retain moisture in considerable degree and the first type is most fertile.

Ujjain is the prime pilgrim centre of Mālwā and is an important knot in the network of sacred Hindu sites. Mahākāl temple is the biggest temple of Ujjain. It is one of the four *kumbha melā* sites. And Ujjain is situated on the east bank of the river

Śiprā. Śiprā is *uttarvāhinī* and is one of the holy rivers of India. Again Ujjain is one of the seven most sacred cities. It lies about sixty kilometres north-west of Indore, the commercial capital of Mālwā. Ujjain is the place where there are a number of Mālwī folk drama groups. The holy city has a history of a few thousand years. So, it has been found to be the most suitable centre for the present study. The Mālwī spoken in Ujjain is considered as pure and literary. The literary tradition of Mālwī has been preserved, developed and nourished in this holy city. It is the centre of literary activities. One of the oldest universities is situated in this city. It was the prime place for astronomical studies.

In Emperor Aśoka's extensive empire (3rd century BC), the spoken language was Pāli. The language varied from province to province — from Indus to Ganges it was Punjābī, in Bengal and other eastern states it was Magadhī, and in Mālwā and the country north of Satpuḍā hills it was Ujjainī. The variation lies in the use of *r*, *l*, *s* and *ś*. While the Punjābī words retain *r* and *s*, the Magadhī substitutes *l* and *ś* for them. Ujjainī retains all of them. Thus 'Rājā' in Punjābī is 'Lāgā' in Magadhī. Ujjainī retains both 'Rejā' as well as 'Lāje', 'Asoka' and 'Aśoka', and 'Śiprā' and 'Siprā'. Mālwī shares many words with Mewārī on the north and Nimaḍī on the south. But it is distinct from these in tone and pronunciation.

Ujjain is longish rectangular in shape and divided into two halves — the city and the residency area. The city area is the old part comprising the portion between the railway-track and the river. This houses the major temples including Mahākāleśvar temple. The residency area is on the south of the rail-track. The city area is congested and the houses are very old. After maping its sacred points we find that its form resembles roughly a *Śivaliṅga* bounded by the holy river, Śipra. According to 1991 census figures, it has a population of more than three-and-a-half lakhs. The following table depicts the population variation during the last ninety years.

Year	*Growth rate*	*Total population*
1901	—	39892
1911	– 1.5	39295
1921	+ 11.7	43908
1931	+ 24.5	53779
1941	+ 48.7	80709
1951	+ 59.7	129817
1961	+ 11.0	144161
1971	+ 44.7	208561
1981	—	282203
1991	—	362266

Ujjain is in central Mālwā. It has regular links with other cities and towns of Mālwā as well as with those of Rājasthān, Gujarāt and Mahārāṣṭra. Buses ply on a regular basis. Besides, there are railway links connecting Ujjain, Ratlām, Guṇā and the State capital, Bhopāl. It is linked with Bhopāl through railroad and state highways. To tackle the rush, there is an efficient bus service between Ujjain and Indore. Besides, Ujjain comes under the jurisdiction of the All India Radio of Indore. From Ujjain two daily newspapers are published in addition to some periodicals. The city is connected with Ratlām by both broad gauge and metre gauge links.

VI

This work is a result of varied efforts. A reconnoitre tour was conducted in early 1978. The original fieldwork was done from 1978 to 1981 in several spells. For the collection of data, standard anthropological techniques were employed. The main emphasis was given on open-ended interviews: key informants have been interviewed and genealogies have been collected. A number of rituals were observed. Fieldwork was conducted in different seasons of the year which helped to observe various rituals from a close distance. A few biographies have also been collected.

2

The Historical Background

MĀLWĀ is the ancient Avantī and Ujjain is the ancient Avantikā or Ujjayinī. The traditional trade routes traversed this region. Ujjain for ages has been an important knot in the north-south and east-west trade through the ports of Gujarāt coast. India had trade ties with the Middle East and the imported goods were channelled to the inland markets through various trade centres. Magadh was then one of the most prominent kingdoms. Ujjain and Vidiśā were the important centres enroute from the Gujarāt ports to Magadh. Again, people from the south used to go to Vārāṇasī touching Maheśvar or ancient Māhiṣmatī, Ujjain, and Vidiśā. Ujjain has found mention in the *Purāṇas*, the great epics and other religious texts. In this chapter an attempt has been made to discuss in brief the historical background of Avantī (Mālwā) and Avantikā (Ujjayinī).

Avantī has had an eventful history partly because it provided by far the best route from northern India to Deccan and so attracted the conquerors. The country is fertile and has supported prosperous kingdoms. Much of the history of Mālwā can be connected with Ujjain, which is one of the most ancient and sacred cities of the area. There are other cities of minor historical importance such as Māṇḍu and Dhār. Ujjain came into prominence and retained its supremacy as the urban centre till the emergence of Indore as the capital of the Holkar state. Little by little, Indore has developed into a modern city and the largest city of the province. But Ujjain has retained its status as a pilgrim centre.

Ujjain is one of the seven sacred cities of antiquity. It reached its zenith as the capital of the legendary King Vikramāditya. During his rule it enjoyed a golden age of prosperity. The city stands at sixteen hundred and seventy-eight feet height above mean sea level. The era which is followed in the area (which begins fifty-seven years before the Christian era) is derived from Vikramāditya's name. Ujjain existed in every *yuga* and was known by the following names — Kanakśṛṅga (house with gold coloured or plated tops), Kuśasthalī (place where a special variety of grass grows), Padmāvatī (full of lotuses), Kumudvatī (abundance of flowers), Amarāvatī (place where the immortal lives), Viśālā (great, large in size), Pratikalpa (existed in various periods), Ujjayinī (named in commemoration of Lord Śiva's triumph over the demon Tripurī), and Avantikā (capital of Avantī)

Ujjain was a seat of learning in ancient days. Śrī Kṛṣṇa and his brother Balarāma lived here at the *āśram* of Sāndīpanī and learnt *the Vedas*, *Vedānta* philosophy and archery. There are memorials and places related to Śrī Kṛṣṇa and Sāndīpanī. In the *Vedas* there is no mention of Ujjain. This does not deny the existence of the town in that period. The *ṛṣis* of the ancient days, during the compilation of the *Vedas*, came from Hindu-Kuśa in the north and reached only as far as Brahmavarta (Bithen). They did not cross the Chambal nor did they make any mention of any town south of this river. Ujjain has found mention in the writings of Ptolemy, and also in the writings of *Periplus* of the Erythrean sea. Ptolemy referred to it as Ozone. To the Greeks and Romans it was known as Urain. The Chinese referred to it as Wu-she-Yen-na or Ujayana. Yuan Chwang visited Ujjain in 641 AD.

Avantī in the early days was inhabited by a tribe whom Abul Fazal in his *Āin-ī-Akbarī* calls 'Hihayas' and the Cambridge

History of India calls Haihayas. It is not sure whether both the groups are the same because both were descended from the Yadu race. They have been connected with the Hūṇas (Wilson). According to the *Viṣṇu Purāna*, the Avantas, Aśmakas, and Vitihotras were the descendants of the Yadu race and they inhabited the country before the seventh century BC. They interdined, intermarried and intermixed and in course of time, the whole tribe acquired the name of Avantas.

From the *Purāṇas* and other sources, we know that the Haihaya had their capital at Māhiṣmatī. Sahaśrajit who was also known as Arjuna Kārtavīrya was a mighty king of the Haihayas. He defeated the great demon king Rāvaṇa. *Parasurāma*, the brahman warrior defeated and killed Sahaśrajīt at Māhiṣmatī. Due to the repeated attacks from the Nāgas and Puṇyajanas (*rākṣasas*) coming from the east and south, the Haihayas shifted to the north. The Nāgas who were defeated by the Haihayas became powerful. Jayadhvaja, a son of Sahaśrajīt, crossed the Vindhyas and settled in the plains of Mālwā, and founded the city of Mālwā. The period is about twelve hundred years before the Mahābhārata war. According to the *Viṣnu Purāṇa*, Śaurasena, the twelfth in descent from Yadu, married Marīśa and he begot her ten sons and five daughters. The youngest of them, Rājādhī-devī, was married to a king of Avantī. She had two sons, Vinda and Anuvinda, and a daughter Mātṛvinda. In *Mahābhārata, Udyogparva* a mention is made of these two princes who took the side of the Kauravas. Mātṛvinda was married to Śrī Kṛṣṇa. The date of the *Mahābhārata* is a subject of controversy and there is little scope to deal with this issue here. It varies from 3102 BC to 1197 BC. According to the *Śatapatha Brāhmaṇa, kaliyuga* began in 3101 BC. Megasthenes has supported this date in his writing. Except Varāhamihira, all the astronomers of India have agreed to this date. The war took place in 3102 BC (C.V. Vaidya) and ended in *mārgaśīrṣa* or December about three months before the onset of *kaliyuga*. It was fought at the close of *dvāparyuga*.

Śrī Kṛṣṇa has been accepted by the historians as Heracles of Greek history. Tilak identifies Dionysus with Daxinayana Manu and Hiracles and Sandrokotas as Śrī Kṛṣṇa and Candragupta. There were 153 generations from Dionysus to Candragupta and Dionysus was fifteen generations earlier than Śrī Kṛṣṇa. Taking twenty years as the average of each reign we have an approximate period of 2760 years separating Śrī Kṛṣṇa and Candragupta. Candragupta's date is 312 BC so we get the approximate date of Śrī Kṛṣṇa as 3071 BC. This tallies approximately with the date of the great war suggested by C.V. Vaidya.

In the *Dharmasutra* of Baudhāyana, there is a mention of Avantī and Baudhāyana, who lived between 1400 and 800 BC. Pāṇini makes a mention of Avantī in his *Aṣṭādhyāyī*. Pocock in his *India in Greece* says that the Avantas distinguished themselves in the Trojan war. Senajīt of the Haihayas is said to have founded his kingdom at Avanti and R.C. Datta places Senajīt at the end of the twelfth century BC. He assigns 1105 BC as the date of the foundation of the kingdom of Avantī. India at this time was divided into sixteen kingdoms. Among these, Magadh, Kośala, Vatsa and Avantī were the *mahājanapadas* and their capitals were respectively, Rājagṛha, Śrāvastī, Kauśāmbī and Avantikā.

King Pradyot ascended the throne of Ujjain in 527 BC. He was a contemporary of Gautam Buddha, Mahāvīra, and Bimbīsār of Śimnāga dynasty. His daughter Vāsavadattā fled with her teacher Udayana in captivity. Udayana was then king of Kauśāmbī. Bhāsa made this story the basis of his drama *Svapnavāsavadattam* and Kālidāsa made a mention of this episode in his *Meghdūta*. During Palaka's rule, Cārudatta and Vasantsenā, the hero and heroine of the famous drama, *Mṛcchakaṭikam* (the clay cart) lived here.

For the advantage of description, the whole period of history can be divided into some stages. Aśoka to Bhoja (286 BC to AD

1060) was the period of Avantī's prosperity. Bindusār, the son of Candragupta of the Maurya dynasty, invaded Ujjain in 286 BC. He kept it as a separate province and posted his son Aśoka as *uparājā.* It consisted of the area from Taxila to Ujjain. Then it was a centre for pilgrimage and also the seat of Indian astronomical studies, and longitudes were computed from its meridian. Aśoka as the king of Pāṭaliputra posted one of his sons here. In Aśoka's time, Paṭnā, Taxila, Allāhābād and Ujjain were the principal towns under the Maurya monarchy. Aśoka found a college for astronomy and astrology at Ujjain. The Buddhist gatherings were held here every third year under the royal patronage. There was a Buddhist monastery in the name of Dakṣiṇagiri, which was also a centre of commerce. Sea commerce was maintained with Mesopotamia and Egypt through the Persian Gulf and the Red Sea. The parts of the west coast were connected with Magadha through Ujjain. It is claimed that the Bhairavgarh Jail was originally constructed by Emperor Aśoka. Aśoka died in the third century BC and was followed by some weak monarchs. In 184 BC Avantī came under the Śuṅga dynasty and was ruled by the founder of this dynasty, Puṣyamitra. After him, his son Agnimitra ascended the throne. They were followed by the Kāṇva dynasty at Pāṭaliputra. But Avantikā no longer remained under Kāṇva rule. Around this time, the Mālavas from Rājasthān and south Punjāb invaded Avantī and founded their monarchy.

The Mālavas lived by the profession of arms and are identical with the Malloi tribe conquered by Alexander. Being subject to repeated attacks of the Scythians and Bactrian Greeks, this group came down to Avantī and settled there. This happened around the first century BC. It is owing to the settlement of the Mālavas here that the country of Avantī came to be called Mālwā. Gandharvasena was the first Mālwā king of Avantī. The legendary King Vikramāditya succeeded Gandharvasena and his history is full of mystery. He is the ideal ruler. Alexander Dow in his *History of Hindusthan* has depicted him as one of the most renowned characters of Indian history. "In policy, justice and wisdom he had no equal. He defeated the first tribe of the Śakas in Punjāb and assumed the title of Śakarī and made Ujjain his capital. In art, literature and mathematics Ujjain reached its peak under him. The Mālavas ruled Ujjain for about a century. Gardabhilā, the last of the Mālavas was defeated by the Śaka-Śatrapas of Gujarat and Kaṭhiāwāḍ. The first king who defeated Gardabhilā belonged to the Bactrian Greeks. They ruled in different parts of India. They were popularly known as Yavanas (etymologically Ionions and originally meaning Asiatic Greeks). The original notions heard about the Greeks came through Ionion traders and hence the word for Greeks in Sanskrit is Yavaṇa. The Śaka-Śatrapas (or Kṣatrapas) ruled till 388 AD. Rudrasinha, the last of the Śakas was killed by Candragupta II of the Gupta dynasty in disguise and Ujjain came under Gupta rule.

Candragupta assumed the title of Vikramāditya and made Ujjain his summer capital. Fahien, the Chinese traveller, toured Mālwā during his rule and described the country of 'warm and equable' climate. The Hūṇas followed the Gupta rulers. On their coins were inscribed *jayatu-vṛṣa-dhvajaḥ* which suggest that they were *Śaivas*. *Liṅgas* of Gupta date are mainly of huge and rugged stones. It is said that the original Mahākāleśvar temple was constructed during the rule of Vikramāditya and it was a huge one thickly studded with gems. During the rule of the Hūṇas, Śaivism flourished in the area. They were war-like and hard-hearted. The Hūṇas snatched Mālwā from Bālāditya of the Gupta dynasty around 492 AD. In 533 AD Yaśodarman defeated Mihirkula of the Hūṇas and annexed Ujjain to Gupta kingdom. But Mahāsengupta, the Governor of Ujjain, declared himself independent about 600 AD. His son Devagupta killed Gṛhavarman, the King of Kannauj and kept queen Rājaśrī in captivity. Rājaśrī's brother Harṣavardhana, the Thāneśvar King defeated Devagupta and annexed both Avantī and Kannauj to his kingdom. Harṣa was a follower of Buddhism while Yuan-Chwang visited Ujjain. He was followed by the Pratihārs whose rule lasted till 946 AD. The Parmāras came from Ābu and invaded Mālwā and established their monarchy at Ujjain. Among the Parmār rulers Muñjadeo and Bhoja were prominent. It is said about them that they wielded the pen and sword with equal facility. Muñja ruled from 973 to 997 AD and Bhoja from 1010 to 1060 AD. During their rule, there was a great revival of enthusiasm in temple construction under royal patronage. Probably they were in favour of Śaivism and a particular tradition of Śiva temple is assigned to the Parmārs. The Mahākāleśvar temple was repaired and renovated. All over Mālwā many temples came up during this period. King Bhoja shifted his capital to Dhārnagarī or Dhār and left Ujjain unprotected and uncared for. During this period the interest in art, literature and temple construction flourished under the royal patronage.

Jayasinha to Mohammad Śāh (1060 to 1732) is the period of ruin and downfall of Ujjain and constant disturbances in Mālwā. The successors of Bhoja ruled till 1290 AD. In 1235 AD Sultān Iltutmish of the Slave dynasty of Delhi attacked the city. He pulled down the Mahākāl temple, where one idgāh came up and destroyed the palaces and gardens. He took away with him the jewellery and the golden image of Vikramāditya. In 1291 Jalāl-ud-dīn Firozśāh Khilji of Delhi invaded Ujjain and two years later, invaded it again. This was followed by an invasion by Alā-ud-dīn Khiljī. The Khiljīs ruled Mālwā from 1291 to 1321 AD.

The Tughlaks ruled Mālwā from 1322 to 1400. In 1367 Dilāwar Khān Ghorī, the Governor of Ujjain built *Ām Khās* palace on the bank of Rudra Sāgar. The ruins are still visible. He turned a Jain or Buddhist *vihār* into a mosque which is known as *binā-nīb-kī-masjid*. In 1401 Dilāwar Khān declared himself as Sultān of Mālwā. His successor, Husāng Śāh, shifted the capital to Māṇḍu around 1408. In 1435 Mohammad Khiljī ascended the throne. He was succeeded by Ghyās-ud-dīn in 1469. After him Nasīr-ud-dīn became Sultān of Mālwā in 1501. He destroyed the temple dedicated to Sūrya which stood in the midstream of Śiprā and built a water palace, which is now known as Kāliādeh Palace. In 1526 Bahādur Śāh of Gujarāt captured Mālwā. Humāyun, the Mughal, seized Mālwā from Bahādur Śāh. It was captured by Mohammad Khān Kāder of Canderī and was recaptured by the Mughals in 1543. The Governor, Sujāwar Khān, kept his capital at Ujjain till 1554. His successor, Bājbahādur, shifted the capital to Māṇḍu. He was engrossed in his queen Rūpamatī and neglected the administration. Emperor Akbar dethroned him in 1564 and shifted the capital to Ujjain. There was stability during the reign of Muhammad Śāh and in 1720 or 1722 Jaisinha of Jaipur became the governor of Mālwā. He built an observatory in Jaisingpura on the Śiprā bank.

In 1690 the Marāṭhā horses crossed the Narmadā but it was only in 1723 that they got a firm footing in some parts of Mālwā. The Mughal power could not resist the inroads of Marāṭhās from the Deccan. In 1728 Scindia acquired more area around Ujjain and under the orders of Peśawā Bājīrāo began to collect *cauth* in Mālwā. By 1732 Pēśawā became the supreme power in Mālwā. After their massacre at the war of Pānīpat with Ahmad Śāh-Durrānī they settled at Mālwā. Peśawā distributed the Mālwā area among his three Sardārs — Holkar, Scindia and Powār. Holkar became the chief of Indore state, Powār got Dhār and Dewās. Ujjain and part of Mālwā fell to the lot of Rāṇojī Scindia.

Marāṭhā rule continued from 1732 to 1949. Ujjain was the capital of Sindhe state. Rāṇojī remained mostly away, fighting wars for the Peśawā. His dewān, Rāmcandra Mulhār Sukhtankar, popularly known as Rāmcandra *bābā*, was in charge of administration. Rāmcandra made a concerted effort to rebuild the city. The Mahākāl temple of today has been constructed under the supervision of Rāmcandra. Several temples were renovated, reconstructed and added. These temples received royal patronage. Funds were arranged for maintenance and the priestly class were also brought from the Deccan. Rāṇojī was a strong pillar of Marāṭhā power. He died in 1743 near Sujhālpur. Jayappā succeeded him and was later killed at Nāgore. His son Jānkojī ascended the throne. After his death, Mahādjī, the youngest son of Rāṇojī and the only survivor in direct line, became ruler in 1761. He was a great warrior and fought battles with the Rohillās, Sikhs, Rājpūts and others from Paṭiālā in the north to Mysore in the south. He extended his territory up to the south bank of Yamunā annexing Gwālior, Āgrā and Mathurā. During his rule also there was construction of temples. Mahādjī was the most powerful prince of the Marāṭhā confederacy. During his reign Ujjain was rich and flourishing. He died in 1794. Hallet, the European traveller who visited Ujjain in 1785, described it as a town of beautiful buildings with a central market.

As Ujjain was developed by the Scindias, Maheśvar, the first capital of the Holkars, was developed by the Holkars. Incidentally, Maheśvar (ancient Māhiṣmatī) is also a place of Śiva-worship. Several temples were constructed and renovated. Ahilyābāī Holkar, a queen of Holkar state, was mainly responsible for temple construction.

Mahādjī Scindia was succeeded by Daulatrāo, the adopted son. During this period the friction between Holkar and Scindia was at its peak. Malhār Rāo Holkar looted Ujjain twice. This and the removal of the capital to Gwālior in 1810 hindered the progress of Ujjain till Bāyājībāī, widow of Daulatrāo, made Ujjain her residence during Jiayājirāo's minority. She lived here from 1847 to 1906. She, like Ahilyābāī Holkar, was a religious lady who got Gopāl Mandir and a few other temples constructed. During the rule of Mādhavarāo, modern amenities like water works (centralised), electricity, wider roads, clubs and other came up. A graduate college was also established. Mādhavarāo died in 1925.

During the British rule, the boundaries of Holkar, Gwālior, Dewās and Dhār states were frozen and there was no infighting.

Following India's independence, the State Department of the Union Government persuaded the princely states to join the Indian Republic. Accordingly in May 1948, Gwālior state along with twenty-five other small states joined the Indian Union. They became part of the erstwhile state of Madhya Bhārat. The states included Gwālior, Indore, Dewās Union, Dewar Senior, Ratlām, Alirājpur, Barwani, Jhābua, Khilchipur, Narsingarh, Jāmiā, Jāorā, Kuruwai, Mahammadgarh, Pettari, Sailana, Siteman, Jabet, Kāṭhiāwāḍ, Mothwar, Rājgarh, and Nīm Kherā. On 1st November 1956, Madhya Pradesh State was formed according to the recommendations of the State Reorganisation Commission of 1955. The Avantī of ancient days or Mālwā became a part of the largest state of the country, Madhya Pradesh.

During the long historical period, the political boundaries changed with the dynasties. But largely it remained undisturbed due to its geographical features. Along with the raiders and invaders, people of diverse origin entered the tableland and settled here. Not only the warriors but also the service groups came with them. Several groups of Marāṭhā brāhmaṇas settled here besides some Marāṭhā army chiefs or *sardārs*. The different populations have come and have been assimilated in the area.

The present town differs from the ancient Avantikā or Ujjain in many respects. The area around Mahākāl temple was known as Mahākālvana. The site of the ancient town which is to the north of Mahākāl temple is now a barren area. It is on a high mound along the bank of Śiprā and is locally known as Garh. It seems that the town and the forest (Mahākālvana) of old days have exchanged their places. The area around Mahākāl temple is now the busiest place and is the commercial centre of the city. It had regular links with Broach, Cāmbay and other ports. The market bears the testimony of olden days. It is said that in the early days some natural calamity like flood or earthquakes had ruined the city or a major part of it.

The tradition of learning continues to be maintained. There are *Veda Pāṭhaśālās*, Sanskrit colleges and the oldest University of Mālwā. People feel proud to mention the nine gems of King Vikram's court. The gems were specialised in different fields, such as Dhanvantari, Kṣapanak, Amarsinha, Śanku, Betāl Bhaṭṭa, Kālidās, Ghaṭakarpar, Varāhamihira and Bararuchi. A number of schools, art colleges and other educational institutes provide facilities to the urbanites and people from nearby rural areas.

The present city is divided into two sections — the city which comprises the area north of the railway track and residency area on the south of the railway track. The former presidency area is developing fast with a cosmopolitan population and is less congested. There is only one major temple here. Free Ganj is the main shopping centre for this sector. The city area is very congested with narrow lanes, and it has the major temples. In each lane there may be a temple and Chatrī Cowk is the heart of this sector. The wholesale markets, dealing in various commodities, are here. This stretches from the railway station to Śiprā *ghāṭs*. The famous Mahākāl temple is in this sector.

The Ujjain of today has a diverse population. There is a predominance of priestly groups and other specialists who perform *pūjā* or rites for the pilgrims. There is a big group of *tīrtha purohits* who have migrated to Ujjain from various places of Rājasthān and Gujarāt. Prominent among the brāhmaṇa groups are Audeech, Gujar Gaur, Śrī Gaur, Adya Gaur, Nārāyaṇadeva and Chenati groups (they include Dadhiet, Śāikhwāls, Sārasvat, Gaur, Pārīk and Khaṇḍelwāl). Besides, several Mahārāṣṭrian brāhmaṇas and some from the Telengānā area came here with their Marāṭhā masters and they are known as Dakṣiṇī brāhmaṇa and Telaṅga brāhmaṇa respectively. *Banyās* include the traditional groups like Agarwāls, Oswāls, Māheśvarīs, etc. Sindhī traders have also settled here. A large portion of trade is controlled by the Bohrās who are Muslims. They are bilingual and speak Gujarātī as well as Mālwī. Farmer castes include Rājpūt, Khāti, Kulmī, Kalota, Patidār, Kunbī, etc. Mālī are the flower growers and Bhoi, the fishermen are now engaged in trade of *bel* leaves. The scheduled castes such as Balai, Camār, Mehtar, Bāgrī, Dhanuk, Naṭ, etc. are important groups. Then there are service castes. Some groups of service castes come from adjacent states and are known as Pardeśī Kumhār or Lohār. They enjoy a lower status than those of Mālwā. Most of the clean castes have their caste *dharmśālā*s and temples in Ujjain. Normally each caste *dharmaśālā* has a temple inside it which also provides cheap accommodation to caste students. During big religious fairs the pilgrims reside in their respective caste *dharmaśālā*s and are provided with other facilities like kitchenware and space for cooking. Some provide food at concessional rates.

In the present attempt, we are concentrating on the Hindu temples only. Special emphasis is on Śiva temples. Lord Mahākāl is one form of Lord Śiva and he is the tutelary god of Ujjain. So Mahākāl temple has been studied in detail with special reference to its rituals.

3

The City of Temples

THE temple of Lord Mahākāl and the *kumbha melā* are the two important reasons why Ujjain is one of the most important centres of pilgrimage. Besides the Mahākāl temple, however, there are a number of temples dedicated to different gods and goddesses of the Hindu pantheon as well as some historical places and shrines. A number of fairs are held and rituals performed in Ujjain, which attract all kinds of people in general and professionals, in particular. The ascetics exist in a large number in Ujjain and they have their *akhāḍās*. Ujjain has some special features. It is a *tīrtha* which rids one of sins and purifies the soul. It is also a *vana*, as the Mahākālvana was there. It is believed that the *vana* is the best place for meditation and thinking. There is a Śakti Pīṭha in Ujjain. It is the site of the *kumbha melā* — the congregation of great souls. There are *śmaśāns*, and a dip in the holy river Śiprā helps one avoid the cycle of rebirth and offers *mukti* (salvation). Ujjain is the site of one of the twelve *jyotirliṅgas*. Mahākāleśvar, one of the twelve such *liṅgas*, has made this ancient city a pilgrim centre distinct from others. Lord Mahākāl is the ruling deity of Ujjain, the ancient Avantikā.

The factors other than the *kumbha melā* which have contributed to Ujjain's sacredness have been considered in this chapter. In the next chapter the Mahākāleśvar temple has been dealt with in detail.

The various temples dedicated to different gods and goddesses can be grouped under five principle categories depending on the deities they are dedicated to. One group of temples is dedicated to Lord Viṣṇu and his various incarnations. There are *Vaiṣṇava* institutions, *akhāḍās* and sacred spots. Some temples are dedicated to the mother goddess and her different forms. The influence of the Śakti cult is strong here. The third group of temples belongs to Gaṇapati and celestial bodies like planets. The fourth group is dedicated to various gods and goddesses of the local tradition or lesser deities. And the final group belongs to the Śaivite group. We will discuss the first four groups and the last group, only marginally. Not all the temples will be discussed as there is little scope for this. The most popular ones have been taken here as examples.

The most important place for the Vaiṣṇavites in Ujjain is the Aṅkpaṭ area which is known as Aṅkpaṭ Kṣetra (Lord Śrī Kṛṣṇa used to clean the slates in the tank here and so the name Aṅkpaṭ). During the *kumbha melā* the *Vaiṣṇava* ascetics camp at this place. Most of the *Vaiṣṇava akhāḍās* are located here. Of the various temples, an important one is the Sāndīpanī *āśram*. It is said that it is the same place where Saint Sāndīpanī, the teacher of Lord Śrī Kṛṣṇa, used to live. After coming from Kāśī, he settled in his *āśram* here. Lord Śrī Kṛṣṇa and his elder brother Balarāma stayed here to learn the *Veda* and other religious texts, and to take lessons in archery. The area is about six kilometres from Chatrī Cowk, the central thoroughfare of the city. It is on the road leading to the Maṅgalnāth temple. Besides, there are two Śiva temples and one of these is the *Caurāsī Liṅga* of Ujjain. There is a boundary wall which is in a dilapidated condition. Adjacent to Sāndīpanī *āśram* is the *baiṭhak* of the *Vaiṣṇava* saint, Ballabhācārya. He has eighty-four such *baiṭhaks* or centres in the country. It is said that the saint meditated under the *pīpal* tree here. Hence, a temple has been constructed. There is a hall for religious discourses and a *dharamśālā.* A trust looks after the temples and this *baiṭhak* of Ballabha *sampradāya.* The expenses are borne by this *sampradāya.* On the south of the *baiṭhak*, there is a temple of Citragupta, the divine recorder. This complex has two sacred lakes, Puruṣottam Sāgar and Śolā Sāgar. Sāndīpanī *āśram* is on the east bank of Puruṣottam Sāgar. Puruṣottam Sāgar is reasonably big though it is mostly dry and shallow (it is filled with silt due to its shallowness). During *adhikmās* people come here to bathe and offer *pūjā* at the neighbouring temples.

On the south bank of Puruṣottam Sāgar is the twin temple of Rām-Janārdan. Both are identical in structure. One is dedicated to Lord Śrī Rāma, younger brother Lakṣmaṇa, consort Sitā and the other temple to Lord Kṛṣṇa Janārdana. Both the temples face north. In front of these temples there is a *kuṇḍa.* The shrine of Lord Bhairava is in this *kuṇḍa.* To the right of these temples, near the lake, there is a Śiva temple. Behind the Janārdana temple, a temple of Lord Hanumān has been constructed recently. A *dharmaśālā* has also come up where the devotees can halt for a day or so. A watchman has been employed to look after the area and the gate of the boundary wall opens into the road leading to Bhairavagarh. There is a trust which looks after these two temples and the Sāndīpanī *āśram,* and donations come in regularly from Indore and Gwālior for their maintenance and payments to *pujārīs*. Fixed deposits and land grants are provided for the temple servants. Of the two priests, one belongs to the Gūjargauḍ group and the other to the Śrīgauḍ group. The latter is one of the sixteen *pujārīs* of Mahākāleśvar and his *iṣṭadevatā* is Lord Viṣṇu. In addition to this, he has a Rāma temple in his house near Chatrī Cowk. He takes out the *ḍol* (palanquin) as part of the procession on *ḍol egāras* day.

In the vicinity of the Janārdana temple, there is a small temple dedicated to Lord Govardhan. It is said that Lord Rāma on his way back to Ayodhyā after killing the demon king Rāvaṇa stopped for a night at this place. And so, a temple was constructed in course of time.

The other lake, Śolā Sāgar, is also sacred and there is a Viṣṇu temple on its south bank. During *adhikmās*, people bathe here and make offerings to Lord Viṣṇu. On the *ḍol egāras* day, a huge procession led by the *ḍol* of Gopāl Mandir comes to this place. Offerings are made on behalf of each *ḍol* to this place. There were as many as twenty-five *ḍols* in the *ḍol egāras* procession which was taken out in the year 1979. After making offerings, the procession starts its return journey.

In Ujjain the most important Viṣṇu temple of today is Gopāl Mandir. Chatrī Cowk is a square and the main thoroughfare of the city. It is at the heart of the old sector. The municipal corporation and all the wholesale markets are close to this square. This is the city bus terminal. There is a park with a statue of King Mādhavarāo Scindia of the Gwālior house under a cenotaph. In local terminology, the memorial is called *chatrī* and hence the name Chatrī Cowk. The statue of King Mādhavarāo faces the Gopāl Mandir which is very close to the Chatrī Cowk. The Gopal Mandir was constructed by Baijābāī Scindia, the queen mother of Gwālior state. She was a devoted *Vaiṣṇava* but not apathetic to other temples and shrines. The temple is dedicated to Dwārkādhīśa, King Śrīkrṣṇa. Apart from the temple and the *dharmśālā*, there are the staff quarters which encircle the temple. The image of the principal deity is in the *garbhagṛha*. On the two sides of the Lord are the idols of Rādhā and Rukmiṇī. The marble statue of Baijābāī Scindia is on one side of the Lord. The *sabhāgṛha* is of the Marāṭhā style, with a demarcated central place for the group of singers while the sitting space for the devotees is in the corridor. The temple is at a height of five feet from the base and the image is placed in such a way that it is visible from the road. Those who are in a hurry can have *darśan* from the road and pay their respects. The priest and other staff live inside the temple. There is a trust to manage matters under the overall supervision of the Scindias. The chief of all the Viṣṇu temples is the Gopāl Mandir as it is patronised by the royal house who were once the rulers.

There is another Gopāl Mandir in the Freeganj area. It is smaller and less popular as compared to the former, and it has been constructed by a rich trader. Besides, there are a number of temples dedicated to Lord Viṣṇu and his incarnations. In all the *akhāḍās* there is a temple or place of worship.

It is believed that there are twenty-four *mātṛkās* or mother goddesses in Ujjain, sixty-four *yoginīs* and a number of *devī* temples. In the Garḍh area there is a Kālikā temple which is known as Gaḍh Kālikā. It is said that she was the propitiating goddess of the legendary Kālidāsa (*sevak* of goddess Kālī). The temple is well built having a *garbhagṛha* and *sabhāgṛha*. There is a small *dharmśālā* and the priest lives in a portion of the building. He belongs to the *Nāth* sect and looks after the temple management. He is a *gṛhasthī nāth*. The temple is about five kms from Chatri Cowk. Animal sacrifice is not done here. The priest claims to be a Śakti Pīṭha, but there is nothing concrete to support this view. The other important *devi* temple is on the east bank of Govardhan Sāgar and is popularly known as the temple of *Nagar-koṭ-ki-rānī*. Here also, animal sacrifice is not done. A *sādhu* lives here and looks after the temple. It is said that in Punjab there is a place called Nagarkoṭ where there is a Śakti Pīṭha. The image at the *devī* temple is the replica of the goddess of Nagarkoṭ. The belief is that King Vikram established this image and the deity is the protecting deity of Ujjain *nagar* (city). The Cāmuṇḍā *mātā* temple at the hospital square is one of the popular temples and here, too, animal sacrifice is not done. The temple of *Caunsaṭha Yoginī* (sixty-four *yoginīs*) is in the busy part of the (Nayapura) city. There is a popular legend which says that once these *yoginīs* used to cause turmoil in the city. Each day a person used to be coronated as the king of Ujjain whom these *yoginīs* killed at night. Once King Vikram came to know about it and played a trick. He placed a large quantity of eatables at all the city gates. While entering, the *yoginīs* consumed the food and were jubilant. Vikram appeased them and requested them to stop killing the king of the town. Hence the temple was constructed and offerings are made regularly. It is believed that though these *yoginīs* have stopped killing they still take some lives at the time of the *siṁhastha melā (kumbha melā)*. Traditionally, at this mela, a holy man announced the time of the *kumbha* dip and almost always, the announcer lost his life. This practice has, however, been stopped now. The brāhmaṇa priest makes offerings at this temple.

The *devīs* of *Caubīs Khambā* are also famous. *Caubīs Khambā* is the remnant of the main gate to the Mahākāl area. The structure rests on twenty-four stone pillars. There are two *devī* images on two sides. A Balai priest makes the offerings. The Balai are the most populous Scheduled Caste among those of Mālwā. The Balai people are largely farmers or farm labourers. *Bhūkhī mātā* shrine is the only *devī* shrine on the west bank of Śiprā. Actually on the west bank except for a few stray shrines there is no major temple. It is an *othla* (raised platform) without any wall or tomb and the priests belong to the Balai caste. Only at this place is a goat offering made and sacrifices performed by the Balai *pujārīs*. In no other temple in Ujjain is animal sacrifice in practice. People who take the vow of animal sacrifice do it here. The Balai priest performs it on their behalf.

The most venerated *devī* temple is that of *mātā* Harsiddhi *devī*. It is said that she was the tutelary goddess of King Vikram. The deity is *Vaiṣṇavī* and so, animal sacrifice is prohibited. It is one of the fifty-two Śakti Pīṭhas of India. Here, it is believed that the temple has come up on the spot where the right elbow of Satī once chanced to fall. The temple stands on the west bank of Lake Rudra Sāgar and on the other bank of the lake is the Mahākāl temple complex. The lake is of shallow depth and remains mostly dry. A road runs across the lake for going from one temple to the other. Harsiddhi temple is on the route from the Śiprā *ghāṭ*s to Mahākāl temple. It has a *ghāṭ* in the Rudra Sāgar. The temple has a boundary wall with two gates and a *dharmaśālā* for the pilgrims. There are two sacred *pīpal* trees and the main temple is at the centre of the complex. In front of this is a pair of big *dīpamālikā* and an underground temple dedicated to Annapūrṇā *devī*. The main temple is also used by the visiting saints for meditation. People can have *darśna* through the skylights and there is a narrow staircase for the exclusive use of priests. There are two Bhairavas at the foot of the main *pīpal* tree, and on the left of the temple is a Śiva temple. This is the fifty-sixth of Ujjain's eighty-four *liṅgas*. The main temple stands at an elevation of about five feet. It is well-constructed, and divided into a *garbhagṛha, sabhāgṛha* and front veranda. In the veranda is depicted a tiger, the *vāhan* of the goddess. In the ceiling of the *sabhāgṛha*, the various incarnations of the mother goddess and the *devī yantra* are depicted. Inside the *garbhagṛha*, there are nine other goddesses in addition to Harsiddhi *mātā*. Thus all the ten incarnations are there, though there is hardly any recognisible iconographical difference as all are under the thick cover of vermilion paste. Only the sizes of the images differ. The priests are the *daśnāmī grhasthī* and they have served the temple for generations.

Janmāṣṭamī, Rāmanavamī and *Holī* are important festivals in Viṣṇu temples. In *devī* temples, on the other hand, *Daśaharā* and *Dīwālī* are important festivals. Both *Caitī* and *Kuār Daśaharā* are important festivals in all *devī* temples though *Kuār Daśaharā* is the more important one. During *Dīwālī* the lamps (earthen) are lighted and decorated on the *dīpamālikās*. Before *Kuār Daśaharā* Harsiddhi *mātā* temple is cleaned and decorated and a fair is held at the temple. A procession is taken out on the *navamī* day and the palanquin of Harsiddhi *mātā* remains in front followed by those of other temples. Harsiddhi mātā is most respected and hers is the chief *devī* temple in Ujjain.

There are six principal Vināyakas in Ujjain and one of them is in the Mahākāl complex. Others are distributed in different parts of the city. Vināyaka, popularly known as Gaṇapati, is worshipped prior to any *śubhakarma* (auspicious rite) or new venture for success. The chief Gaṇapati temple is that of Cintāman Gaṇapati of Jawasia village. It is about five kms from Chatrī Cowk and the Ujjain-Candravatīganj meter gauge link passes through this village. In response to the demand of the devotees, a flag station has also come up. The temple has a *garbhagṛha* and a *sabhāgṛha.* There is a huge image of Lord Gaṇapati in the *garbhagṛha.* There is a *dharmaśālā* for the pilgrims and a boundary wall. A well exists in the name of *bāṇgaṅgā* and it is believed to have been created by Lakṣmaṇa to satisfy the thirst of Sītā, consort of Lord Rāma. Wednesday is the day of Lord Gaṇapati and the month of *Caitra* is important for the lord. On each Wednesday of the month of *Caitra* (March-April), a fair is held at the temple of Cintāman Gaṇapati at Jawasia village. People from distant places come here. Those who do not drop in at the temple have a view of the temple top and pay their respects. People from Ujjain city area come here for picnics at weekends. In other Gaṇapati temples, special *pūjā* is offered on *Caitra budhvārs*. The other important Gaṇapati temple is *baḍāgaṇeśa*, which is behind the Mahākāl temple on the Harsiddhi road and enroute from Harisiddhi mātā temple. The temple is fairly big with two sections and the front apartment has a huge Gaṇapati idol touching the high ceiling. In the inner portion there are a few sections with idols of Pañcamukhī Hanumān, Lord Śiva, Devī, the planets, a *jhūlā* of Lord Kṛṣṇa and the reading room of Sāndīpanī *ṛṣi.* It is a composite temple and Lord Gaṇeśa is the chief deity of the temple. The temple is quite popular and one of the important temples of Ujjain. It is a private temple constructed by the late Paṇḍit Sankarṣaṇ Vyās. There was also a *ved pāṭhśālā* here. However, in importance, Cintāman Gaṇapati is on top of the list of temples dedicated to Lord Gaṇeśa.

Of the Śiva temples, Mahākāl is the largest and most important. He is the supreme Lord of Ujjain. The temple has several other small temples and is a complex which stands on the east bank of Rudra Sāgar lake on the southern precincts of the city. The area was known as Mahākālvana in the *purāṇik* age. The Rudra Sāgar lake which is the biggest of all the sacred lakes in the city has probably come up due to the change of course of the river Śiprā. There are regular buses to reach the temple gate and other conveyance are also easily available. Lord Mahākāleśvar is represented in the *liṅga* form and it is one of the twelve *jyotirliṅgas* of India. Various gods and goddesses, and *grahas* and other planets have been represented here in *liṅga* form. In the version of a local *ācārya*, Ujjain is *liṅgamaya* (full of *liṅgas*), so much so that they cannot be counted. There is no end of Śiva temples and the *caurāsī liṅgas* or the eighty-four *liṅgas* of Ujjain are sacred and famous. They are the various incarnations of Lord Śiva. Besides Mahākāl, Agasteśvar Mahādeva, Nāg Candreśvar and Pāṭāleśvar Mahādeva are important Śiva temples. Except Mahākāl, in all the Śiva *liṅgas* the *jaladhārī* opens in the north. The eighty-four Śiva temples (*caurāsī liṅga*) are distributed all over the city and the pilgrims visit these during a *yātrā*.

Of the temples dedicated to sacred trees, planets and lower deities, *Sidhvaṭ* is one of the most important temples of Ujjain. *Sidhvaṭ* is the sacred banian tree and is one of the four sacred banian trees of India (the *Kalpavṛkṣas*) — *Akṣayvaṭ* of Prayāg, *Baudhvaṭ* of Gayā, *Baṅsivaṭ* of Vṛndāvan and *Sidhvaṭ* of Ujjain. The tree is on the left bank of Śiprā. River Śiprā here has formed a pot hole which is quite deep. There are *ghāṭs* where last rites and rites before or after completion of *tīrthayātrā* (pilgrimage) are performed. There are *tīrtha purohits* who help in performing such rites. The *liṅga* form has been made at the root of the tree, which is worshipped. The place is also known as *Śaktived tīrtha*. It is said that Kārttikeya killed Tārakāsur here and Pārvatī, consort of Lord Śiva, planted this tree. So it is unperishable, and it can provide anything and fulfil any desire. People come here for three purposes — the villagers for curing diseases, the gentry and villagers who are childless and some for the performance of rites. Once a child is born to them, childless couples visit this place with the child to make offerings. They make a *svastik* mark and the natal hair of the new-born is offered. There are two kinds of *tīrtha purohits* — the *paṇḍā* and *kātya*, who are both *brāhmaṇa*.One performs *śubha śrāddha* and the other *aśubha śrāddha*. They do not serve the untouchables. The *śubha śrāddha* (*tripiṇḍa, tīrtha piṇḍa śrāddha, caturdaśī śrāddha*, etc.) are performed by *paṇḍās* and *kātyas* do the *aśubha śrāddha* (*daśva, nāgabali, nārāyaṇabali, kriyākarma*). The *kātya* enjoy a low status and the *śukla* have a high status. In all there are five *ghāṭs*, three on the south of the temple and two on the north of it. One of the southern *ghāṭs* is reserved for ladies and the other two are used for rituals and bathing by the caste Hindus. On the north there is the *harijan ghāṭ* (for scheduled caste people) and the other is the *dhobī ghāṭ* (for washermen). The river flows north, and the *harijan ghāṭ* is at the lower stream and outside the *tīrtha* complex.

The priests belong to the Mauḍ Caturvedī group and their *iṣṭadevī* (tutelary goddess) is Mauḍeśvarī. They migrated from Gujarāt state about eight generations ago. They are *Vaiṣṇavas* and have a *śāligrām* at their houses which is worshipped daily. But as the priest of this temple, they remain like Śaivites. An *akhaṇḍa dhūnī* is maintained by a *daśnāmī gṛhasthī*. Besides this Siddhnātha temple, there are a number of temples which are mostly Śiva temples. Actually it is a group of temples with the Siddhanāth temple as the main one. The *paṇḍās* have their rooms at the *dharamaśālā*. Here there is a temple of Pātāleśvar Mahādeva which is at a depth of about fifteen feet.

Sidhvaṭ has links with the legendary King Vikramāditya. It is said that he achieved salvation here. Kārttikeya, after killing the demon Tārakāsur, was called back by Lord Śiva to Kailāsa as Śiva was pleased with his performance. So those whose last rites are performed here are destined to go to Kailāsa. *Sidhvaṭ* is one of the twenty-eight and eight main *tīrthas* of Ujjain. The funeral rite of the tenth day has to be performed here before performing the same at *Rāmghāṭ*. It is about six kms from Chatrī Cowk and there are regular city buses facilitating movement of the pilgrims.

A little further is the Kāliādah palace in the midstream of river Śiprā. Actually it is on an island where the course of the river bifurcates and joins at a distance. This summer palace, it is said, was originally a Sūrya temple. An image of Lord Sūrya exists and this suggests the tradition of Sun-worship in the area in the past. During Pañca Kośī *yātrā* (taking a round of Ujjain *kṣetra*) the *yātrīs* use the open space here for camping. Light and other arrangements are made for the devotees by the local authorities.

Ujjain is one of the important centres for *Nāth-yogīs*. Several temples are managed by *Nāths*, both *gṛhastha* and *virakta* (*saṁnyāsī*). In villages also the members of the *Nāth panth* (sect) are found. *Māchh* is the traditional folk theatre of Mālwā and Ujjain is the centre where it evolved, modified and flourished. There are many *Māchh sampradāyas* who stage dramas based on local themes as well as on themes from great epics. These *sampradāyas* always have a *Nāth-yogī* as an active member of the troupe and he has some duties to perform.

The *Nāths* believe that there are nine *Nāths* and eighty-four *siddhas*. They are Śaivites and their main centre is Gorakhpur in Bihar. Bhartṛhari was a disciple of the most venerated of the *Nāths*, Guru Gorakhnāth. He was the king and the elder brother of the legendary King Vikram. He left the throne and meditated in a cave nearby, which goes by his name and is known as Bhartṛhari cave. It is on the bank of River Śiprā. Bhartṛhari is considered as one of the nine *Nāths*. Bhartṛhari cave is the main centre of the *Nāth-yogīs* (they are also known as *kanphaṭa-yogī*, as they wear heavy earrings). During *siṁhastha* (*kumbha melā*), *Nāth* mendicants camp at this place. The *mahant* of this centre is known as *pīrjī* who is the head of the *Nāth-yogīs* here. He is a *virakta Nāth*. There are two *gaddīs* here — one of Guru Gorakhnāth and the other of Bhartṛhari. The *gaddī* of Guru Gorakhnāth is at the ground level and two floors are below the ground level. In the lower floor is the place where King Bhartṛhari meditated. At the end of the hall there is a *Śivaliṅga* regularly worshipped by the *mahant*. There are two other *Śivaliṅgas*, dancing Śiva, Bhairavī and other images. A staircase leads down to the lower chamber and it is said that the lower floors might have sunk due to floods in the river Śiprā or because of some other natural calamity. This is a house and not a natural cave. Paśupatināth is considered the propitiating god. Bhartṛhari cave is one of the important places in Ujjain.

Machīndarnāth was the founder of *Nāth sampradāya*. But Guru Gorakhnāth, his disciple, made it popular and had a great number of followers. There is a memorial of Machīndarnāth, about which there are disputes between Muslims and Hindus. Both observe the festivals here. Raṇamukteśvar Śiva temple is another important Śiva temple under the control of the *Nāth-yogīs*. Gaḍkālikā temple also belongs to the *Nāth gṛhasthī* members.

Rāmdās Swāmī was the preceptor of the Marāṭhā King Śivājī. He popularised the worship of Lord Hanumān in the Marāṭhā territory. In each village in Mahārāṣṭra there is a Hanumān temple. Under the Marāṭhā domination, Hanumān-worship became popular. There are a number of Hanumān temples in Ujjain. Hanumān-worship has not penetrated the rural areas much. During the Marāṭha rule, several Marāṭhā groups settled in Ujjain. They constructed several temples for commoners as well as private temples. Some temples are dedicated to Viṭṭhal-Paṇḍharīnāth. He is a deity of regional popularity, and has a great number of followers in Mahārāṣṭra. The *Vārkāri* sect which is a powerful *sampradāya* in Mahārāṣṭra is attached to Lord Viṭṭhal of Paṇḍharpur in Mahārāṣṭra. Some temples have come up under the influence of the immigrant population. There are temples of Śrīnāthjī and Alakdhām that belong to migrants from Rājasthān.

Similarly, there are temples dedicated to deities popular in rural Mālwā. Some of the common temples are those of Lālbāī-Phūlbāī, Śītalāmātā, Ajopāl and other caste deities. Each major caste of Mālwā has a temple of its deity.

The other important group of temples is that of Bhairava or Bherū. There are eight principal Bhairava temples in Ujjain. Besides, there are Bherūs at various *devī* temples, *śmaśān* and other places. Bhairavas are believed to be sons of Lord Śiva or created by him. They are the fighters for Lord Śiva. Mainly there are two Bhairavas — Kālā and Gorā. Kālabhairava is the army chief of Lord Śiva, the principal *gaṇa*. The Kālabhairava temple of Bhairavagarh is the most popular Bhairava temple of Ujjain. It is one of the important temples of this *kṣetra*. It is about seven kms from Chatrī Cowk and is one of the old temples too. The village Bhairavagarh has derived its name from this deity. Bhairavasingh was the builder of this temple which is situated on the left bank of River Śiprā and has a *ghāṭ* called *bhairava-ghāṭ*. The temple has a boundary wall and a big gate. Inside the temple there is a *garbhagṛha* and a *sabhāmaṇḍapa*. The priest belongs to the Mauḍ Caturvedī group and is basically a *Vaiṣṇava*. But in attire and attitude he lives like a *Śaiva* and mostly remains under the spell of liquor. A *gṛhasthī* priest makes offerings to the god and liquor is the main item offered to the deity. A dog is Kālabhairava's companion. There are a number of dogs in the temple precinct and they are never beaten or tortured fearing the curse of the Lord. A fair marks the *bhairūpūnam*-day and a procession is taken out on the *bhairavāṣṭamī*-day. People in large numbers visit the temple. Lord Kālabhairava is all the more feared as he is an angry Lord, and so he has to be kept happy. Behind the main temple there is the temple of Pātāla Bhairava at a depth of about fifteen feet. People do not visit this temple for fear of snakes.

In rural Mālwā every village has more than one Bhairava temple. Bhairava-worship is widely practised. In the Kālabhairava temple there is a *Śivaliṅga* also. The temple faces west. A *nagāḍākhānā* (concert platform) exists above the main entrance but it is not in use. The boundary walls are largely in ruins.

We have already noted that there are some temples dedicated to planets. Of these two are very important — Maṅgalnāth on the northern part of the holy city and Navagraha Mandir, the composite temple of nine planets, on the southernmost point. The Maṅgalnāth temple stands on the right bank of Śiprā. There is a *ghāṭ* for the devotees to bathe and make offerings. It is said that the planet Maṅgal originated here. Special offerings are made on Tuesdays. The planet has been represented in *liṅga* form. There is a *dharmaśālā* where the devotees can stay. The temple is under the control of *daśnāmī gṛhasthī* and it has a *mahant* elected by the *pañca*, who is the priest. Various rituals are performed here. It is one of the important temples and *tīrthas* of Ujjain and actually the last *tīrtha* for the *yātrīs* for *aṣṭatīrthī*. The southernmost temple of Ujjain is the Navagraha temple situated at the confluence of rivers Śiprā and Gambhira. It is famous as *Triveṇī* and is near the entry tax post on the Indore road. There are *ghāṭs* near the temple. Saṅgameśvar Mahādeva temple is quite old and there is a huge *liṅga* in the temple. The planets have been represented in *liṅga* form and devotees mostly come here to make offerings to Lord Śiva. On *śani amāvasyā*-day (dark night on Saturday) there is a fair and people from far and near come to take a dip. They then make offerings to Lord Śani. There are other temples dedicated to planets like Bṛhaspati, but Śani temples are greater in number.

Śmaśān (crematorium) is a need and an essential part of any pilgrim centre. In Ujjain last rites are performed at the Śiprā *ghāṭs* with a view that the deceased will be free from rebirth.

Similarly, if somebody is cremated in a particular *śmaśān* he is supposed to be rid of the cycle of rebirth. In Ujjain there are three *śmaśāns* (cremation grounds) — Cakratīrtha, Okhareśvar and Rājmalghāṭ. Okhareśvar is near the Kāłabhairava temple and it has cemented raised platforms for burning the dead. There is a Śiva temple and the temple of Vikrānt Bhairava, which is linked with King Vikram again. There are arrangements for making a pyre and necessary items are available. People of the west bank of Śiprā use this cremation ground. On the other side is the Rājmalghāṭ which is poorly maintained and where there is no proper arrangement for cremation. The main *śmaśān* among these is, however, the Chakratīrtha which is considered a *tīrtha*. People come here for cremation in maximum numbers. They even come from the villages as it has its own *māhātmya* (veneration). It is very close to the famous Śiprā *ghāṭ*s. There are good arrangements for cremation at all times. Cremation platforms are there at a lower level and there are platforms with shades during the rains. It is on the right bank of Śiprā. There are bathrooms and a *dharamśālā* for the relatives of the deceased to rest for a while. The person who looks after it is a corporator and a *udāsīn gṛhasthī*. An *akhaṇḍa dhūnī* is maintained. Here, dried cowdung and wood for pyre are available on payment. There is a temple of Bhūteśvar Mahādeva which has one of the eighty-four *liṅga*s of Ujjain. Cakratīrtha is said to be as sacred as the famous Maṇikarṇikā *ghāṭ* of Banāras.

In Hindu mythology the river has a special place and there are sacred rivers. Water itself has a role in ritual performance. Water from several *tīrtha*s and sacred rivers are physically brought or supposed to be brought by chanting of *mantra*s for the *pūjā* of several gods and goddesses. There are a number of pilgrim centres on the banks of rivers which are very important for the Hindus. To site a few, we may name Prayāg, Haridvār, Kāśī, Oṁkāreśvar, Nāsik, Sāgar, Ujjain, etc. Sacred rivers can provide *puṇya* if one takes a dip in their holy waters. Śiprā is one such sacred river, on the bank of which Ujjain is situated. Here Śiprā is *uttarvāhinī* (flowing north) and this makes it more sacred. It has found mention in the *Skanda Purāṇa*. Vindhyas is considered as the oldest mountain range in India. A number of temples are there in the Vindhyācal. The Mālwā plateau slopes to the north and so the rivers flow north. This direction is again important because in the north is the great Himālayas which is also the *devālaya* (abode of gods). The offerings which are carried northwards by the river is believed to reach the sacred hill Kailāsa (abode of Lord Śiva) in the Himālayas. Hence the river Śiprā is very sacred and it gives *mukti* (salvation). It takes different forms at different hours where the popular beliefs are concerned. In the morning it flows as river Gaṅgā, during midday it is Sarasvatī, in the afternoon water of all *tīrtha*s come here, and in the night it is the holy Narmadā. About the origin of the river Śiprā, it is believed that once Lord Mahākāl being hungry went on begging. He could not get anything and being tired approached Lord Viṣṇu who also refused and showed the thumb to him. Lord Mahākal got furious and hurt the thumb of Lord Viṣṇu with his *triśūl* (trident). The profuse bleeding of Viṣṇu's thumb took the shape of river Śiprā.

Bathing particularly in sacred lakes or rivers is one way of purification of the body and soul. People take a holy dip in Śiprā at Ujjain on the occasion of *Kārtik pūnam* festival, *somtī* (*amāvasyā* on Monday) or *śani amāvasyā* (*amāvasyā* on Saturday), the *Kumbha melā* and other festivals. After performing the last rites in the holy *ghāṭ*s people bathe and get purified in the holy waters.

River Śiprā flows north to meet the main river Cambal or Carmanvatī near village Sipawar in Jaorā *tehsīl*. Cambal flows into the Yamunā and the Yamunā meets the Gaṅgā at Prayāg. The Śiprā originates in the valley of a hillock a few miles off Indore. Its total length is one hundred and twenty miles and the river does not have a perennial flow. It almost encircles the city of Ujjain with several turnings. At places it has potholes which provide bathing facilities and the temples are mainly near such potholes. At Ujjain the Śiprā is studded with (mainly right bank) temples, shrines, sacred *maṭhs* of varied popularity and importance. There are many temples of ancient antiquity and they are lined with rows of steps of the various *ghāṭs*. People make offerings at the temples and bathe at the *ghāṭs*. Of these a few are very important, such as the Rāmghāṭ. At Rāmghāṭ the last rites are performed and the *bairāgīs* (Vaiṣṇavite saints) during the *kumbha melā* take the holy dip at this *ghāṭ*. On the other bank is the *ghāṭ* of *Dattā Akhāḍā* which is meant for *Śaiva* saints who take the holy dip during the *kumbha melā*. In this row of *ghāṭs* there are a number of Śiva temples of various sizes, historical importance and popularity. Besides Rāmghāṭ, the other important *ghāṭs* are Narsiṁha *ghāṭ*, Piśācamukteśvar *ghāṭ*, Udāsī *ghāṭ*, Gaṅgā *ghāṭ*, Maṅgalnāth *ghāṭ*, Sidhnāth *ghāṭ* and Triveṇī *ghāṭ*.

Besides the river Śiprā, there are seven sacred lakes in Ujjain. Most of these lakes are dry now and some have become an open space having no depression. A few are too shallow to hold water. On the bank of each lake there is a Śiva temple. Rudra Sāgar, the largest lake, is behind the Mahākāleśvar temple. Khīr Sāgar and Puṣkar Sāgar are inside the city. At the site of Khīr Sāgar a stadium has been constructed. Govardhan Sāgar, Viṣṇu Sāgar, Puruṣottam Sāgar and Śolā Sāgar are in the northern part of the city. Ratnākar Sāgar or Undiārā Tālāb is about five kilometres from the city. According to the local almanac, an *adhikmā* comes every three years. During this month on scheduled dates people bathe in specific lakes and make offerings at the temple on its bank. Specific items such as cereals and pulses are given to the brāhmaṇa and the poor as *dāna*. This is done on auspicious occasions. Besides these sacred lakes, there are other small lakes near Ujjain. One such lake is very close to the Cintāman Gaṇapati temple.

In Ujjain there are eighty-four Śiva temples, eight temples of

Bhairavas, eleven of Rudra, twelve of Āditya, twelve Devī temples, twenty-four *mātṛkāṣ* and six of Vināyaka. The festivals of Ujjain can be grouped under two categories — *yātrās* and making offerings. *Parivrajana* or travelling far and wide from one sacred centre to the other was an accepted way of *sādhnā* in the ancient Hindu religious system. The *parivrajana* helped people to come closer to various personalities and it was considered as part of the initiation to sainthood. Perhaps the motive was to exchange views with various groups. There are various types of *yātrās* (travellings) along the course of sacred rivers — travelling from the place of rise of a river to its confluence, visiting *cārdhāma* (four sacred places), visiting various *tīrthas*, etc. Some are prescribed for sainthood and others are for the commoners. Taking a round of some *kṣetras* is considered as necessary to earn *puṇya*. This is called *pañcakośī yātrā*. In Ujjain the principle *yātrās* are *pañcakośī* (taking a round of the *kṣetra* and visiting the four *dvārapālas*), *cāradvāra* (going to four *dvārapāla* temples separately), *Aṣṭatīrthī* (visiting eight or twenty-eight *tīrthas* on Śiprā bank), *nagar pradakṣiṇā* (taking a small round of the city), and *caurāsī liṅga* (visiting eighty-four *liṅgas* of Ujjain). Through *yātrās* people have *darśana* of various gods, bathe and get purified. Another way of *mukti* from *pāpas* or purification is to have a holy dip on auspicious occasions. *Kārtik snān, śani amāvasyā snān, somtī amāvasyā snān* are important. *Kārtik melā* of Ujjain draws people from distant places. They float lighted *dīpa* and then take a bath. During this period a cattle fair is held where asses are sold and purchased. This is the only market for donkey trade in Mālwā. It is believed to have been started by King Gardhavila, King Vikram's successor. *Kumbha melā snān* is the most important *snān*. Some festivals have a direct link to a temple, like *Śivarātri* with Mahākāl and other Śiva temples and *Janmāṣṭamī* with Gopāl Mandir and other *Vaiṣṇava* temples. Besides, there are festivals of local importance, such as *Gangaur, Sañjhā*, Bhairava *pūjan* (Bhairava temples). *Navrātra* is observed in the Devī temple, while the

Gaṇapati festival takes place in Gaṇeśa temples. Some of the festivals are observed by specific temples only. During such festivals, there are fairs at these temples. Festivals are also observed at different levels by various castes and communities. There are immigrants who observe their festivals like the Marāṭhās observe *Hanumān Jayantī* with special significance — a tradition kept alive to provide an identity. The following calendar notes the rituals observed in a year.

Rituals Observed in a Calendar Year
(Vikram Samvat)

Month	***Half***	***Day***	***Ritual***	***Remarks***
Caitra (March-April)	Dark	*Pratipadā*	*Samvatsar Lālbāī Phūlbāī Pūjan*	
		Pañcamī	*Jāmrā* or *Raṅga Pañcamī*	
		Satam	*Silisātam*	
	Bright	*Ekam* to *navamī*	*Cait Navrātri* and *Bārī*	
		Ekam to *Tīj*	*Gangaur*	
		Navamī	*Ram Navamī*	
Baiśākh (April-May)	Dark	*Daśamī* to *Caudas*	*Pañcakośī Yātrā*	
		Amāvasyā	*Mahākāl Darśana*	
	Bright	*Tīj*	*Akṣhay Tṛtīyā*	
		Pūnam	*Siṁhasth Snān*	(*Kumba* every twelve years)
Jyeṣṭha (May-June)	Dark	*Amāvasyā*	*Bār Māvas**	

Month	***Half***	***Day***	***Ritual***	***Remarks***
	Bright	*Sātam*	*Bār Sātam**	
		Daśamī	*Gaṅgā Daśamī*	
		Pūnam	*Rāmnām*	
Āṣāḍha (June-July)	Dark	*Gyāras*	*Dev Sonī*	Beginning of *Cāturmas*
	Bright	*Pūnam*	*Bhātpūjan*	
Srāvaṇ (July-August)	Dark	*Amāvas*	*Devāsā* or *Haryālī**	All *Śrāvaṇ somvār* specially observed in Śiva temples. *Mahākāl savārī* is taken out on each *somvār*
	Bright	*Pañcamī*	*Nāgapañcamī*	
		Pūnam	*Rakṣābandhana, Śrāvaṇī*	
Bhādon (August-September)	Dark	*Tīj*	*Tījmātā**	
		Aṣṭamī	*Janmāṣṭamī*	
		Amāvasyā	*Merī Mātā Pūjan*	At village level by Patel
	Bright	*Bīj*	*Rāmdeo Bābā Pūjan*	
		Tīj	*Hartālikā*	
		Cauth	*Gaṇeśa Cauth*	

Month	**Half**	**Day**	**Ritual**	**Remarks**
		Pañcamī	*Ṛṣi Pañcamī*	
		Chaṭ	*Hal Ṣaṣṭhī*	
		Daśamī	*Tejā Daśamī*	
		Gyāras	*Ḍol Gyāras*	
		Caudas	*Anant Caudas*	
Kuār (September-October)	Dark	*Ekam* to *Amāvasyā*	*Śrāddha Pakṣa*	
		Ekam to *Amāvasyā*	*Sāñjhā Pūjan**	
	Bright	*Ekam* to *Navamī*	*Baripūjā*	
		Ekam to *Navamī*	*Kuār Navrātri, Mātā Pūjan*	
		Daśamī	*Vijay Daśamī*	
		Gyāras to *Pūnam*	*Kālikā Mātā Pūjan**	
		Pūnam	*Garbā, Śārdā Pūjan**	
Kārtik (October-November)	Dark	*Aṭam*	*Karvā Āṭam**	
		Teras	*Dhanteras*	
		Caudas	*Rūp Caudas* or *Narak Caudas*	
		Amāvasyā	*Dīwālī*	
	Bright	*Ekam*	*Annakūṭ, Govardhan Pūjā**	
		Dvij	*Bhāī Dūj*	
		Aṭam	*Gopāṣṭamī*	

Month	Half	Day	Ritual	Remarks
		Navamī	*Awlā Navamī**	Brāhmaṇa couple fed. End of *Cāturmās*
		Gyāras	*Deb Uṭhnī Gyāras*	
		Pūnam	*Kārtik Melā*	
Aghan (November-December)	Dark Bright			
Pauṣa (December-January)	Dark Bright	*Saṅkrāntī*	*Til Saṅkrānti*	
		Pūnam	*Vrata* by unmarried girls*	
Māgh (January-February)	Dark Bright	*Pañcamī*	*Vasant Pañcamī*	
Phāgun (February-March)	Dark Bright	*Caudas* *Pūnam*	*Śivarātri* *Holī*	

* Festivals mainly observed by women or for women only.

The devotees come to Ujjain, one of the seven foremost sacred cities for Hindus in India, mainly for three purposes — making offerings to Lord Mahākāleśvar, taking a holy dip in the river Śiprā and performing purificatory rites. For the priests and other professionals associated with religious activities here, it is a place where they can earn much. Through the ages it has attracted the pilgrims and priests with equal force — one comes for service and the other sells his services. The brāhmaṇa groups from the bordering states of Gujarāt, Rājasthān and also from Mahārāṣṭra came and settled here. From Gujarāt and Rājasthān, the brāhmaṇas came in search of employment. Marāṭhā brāhmaṇas came here with Marāṭhā chiefs and received royal patronage. The main brāhmaṇa groups are Ādi gauḍ, Śrī gauḍ, Gujar gauḍ, Audicya, Nārāyaṇdeva, Bāvisā, Chenāti, Dakṣiṇī (Mahārāṣṭrian brāhmaṇas comprise Kārhaḍi, Deśasth and Kokanesṭh) and Teleṅga (from the river bank of Godāvarī of Telengānā area) brāhmaṇas. The last group has a special reputation as priests. They belong to the *pañca draviḍ* group, having come here under royal patronage as temple priests.

At the Śiprā *ghāṭs* there are two kinds of brāhmaṇas who are known as *tīrtha purohit* (the *paṇḍā* and the *kātya*). Gujar gauḍ, Śrī gauḍ and Audīcya are the *tīrtha purohits*. There are as many as one hundred and fifty-two *tīrtha purohits*. And there is a committee with a president who is called *śukla*. There are a number of registered *paṇḍā* companies and they have their own trademark such as *ḍābbāvālā*, *hātivālā*, *nāharvālā*, etc. They maintain registers for their *jajmāns*, provide food and shelter to their *jajmāns* on payment and make arrangements for *pūjā*. A group of *paṇḍās* remain at the bus stands and railway stations of the city to welcome new *jajmāns*. There are *paṇḍās* at Mahākāl temple who perform *abhiṣeka*, *pūjan*, etc. on payment, sell flowers and other items required in making offerings and also look after the belongings of their *jajmāns*. Besides these *tīrtha purohits*, there are brāhmaṇas who are specialised in other works such as reading and explaining sacred texts, giving religious discourses (*kathāvācaks*), *pāṭh* (recitation) of sacred texts on contract for *jajmāns* at specific temples and guidance for various *yātrās* and ritual performances, *jāpa* (uttering names of specific deities a fixed number of times) according to traditions for the *jajmāns* on payment, *yajña* and other *abhiṣeka pūjan* like *rudrābhiṣek* for the *jajmāns*. A group specialises in recitation of the *Vedas* and in ritual performances and it is in great demand. The *śuklās* (specialised priestly perfomers) get the highest honour. They advise people in the performance of rituals and belong to the *Yajurveda* group. Temples are the places where the *kathāvācaks*, and other brāhmaṇas who recite *jāpa* or *pāṭh* also get their assignments. There are fixed rates for the various services. But rates also vary with the ability and popularity of the performer and the economic standing of the *jajmān*. The brāhmaṇas regularly pour into the city to earn a living.

The religious organisations and *akhāḍās* are important institutions in this pilgrim centre. Brāhmaṇas of several *akhāḍās* of the *Śaiva, Vaiṣṇava* and *Nāth* sects and other religious organisations are at Ujjain. The term *akhāḍā* is derived from *akhaṇḍa* or everlasting. These *akhāḍās* serve several purposes and there are a number of resident ascetics, who provide food and shelter to the travelling ascetics. In an *akhāḍā* preference is always given to the ascetics following its school of religious philosophy. The ascetics live a life of negation which is the core of Hindu asceticism. Such radical asceticism is also a feature of the *akhāḍās* here. Each *akhāḍā* has its own establishment and a temple of its *iṣṭadeva* and other gods and goddesses. An *akhāḍā* provides a model living to the commoner and retains his faith in religion. In the *akhāḍā*, various religious discourses are organised for the common people. During the *kumbha melā*, the *akhāḍās* become very active, since they have to provide food and shelter to their fellow saints and even to ascetics of other sects. These *akhāḍās* have regular contacts with their sister branches in other sacred cities of the country and the link is strongly maintained. The ascetics here attend *kumbha melās* at other venues besides religious congregations at other places, and they also visit other centres even when there is no specific occasion. This way, countrywide communication is maintained between the centres. In addition, they maintain centres in the villages. Saints of a particular philosophy live in a small temple in interior villages and propagate the religious ideas as well as maintain an environment of religiosity. The *akhāḍā* provides moral, material as well as organisational support to these ascetics and saints. In the streets and temples of Ujjain the ascetics are very common. One may find an ascetic performing meditation or *jāpa* or some other religious act which may attract the common people. The activities are on throughout the year, but the extent of involvement, the pomp and show reaches its zenith during the *kumbha melā*.

The saints and ascetics who assemble from all parts of the country during the *kumbha melā* belong to one of the five traditional religious doctrines — Bairāgīs, Gosāīn, Udāsī, Nāth and Aghorī. They are again divided into subordinate orders and sub-orders. Bairāgīs attend the *melā* in large numbers followed by Gosāīns and Udāsīs. Aghorīs are few in number but *Nāthpanthīs* have a good footing here. They are *haṭha-yogī*s, practise abstract meditation with the help of *āsanas*, *prāṇāyāmas* and other rigid methods. The Aghorī is an order of mendicants who are associated with some revolting practices. They have only one centre in Ujjain.

The *akhāḍās* belong to various *sampradāyas*. In the following lines a brief account is given of the manner in which these *akhāḍās* are organised. This is necessary to evaluate the functioning of these institutions. At Ujjain there are followers of the following *sampradāyas*.

Viṣṇu sampradāya	Mādhava Ballabha Nimbārka Rāmānujī Ālwar Sant Nāmdeva Panth Vārkari Panth Kabīr Panth
Gānapatya sampradāya	There are followers but no specific institutions.
Śāktamat	The *Śāktas* divide the subcontinent into

	Viṣṇukrāntā, *Rathakrāntā* and *Asvakrāntā*. At Ujjain there is a *pīṭha* which is one of fifty-two *śakti pīṭhas* scattered in the subcontinent. These fifty-two *pīṭhas* are distributed in three divisions. The ascetics of this *mat* always move with the *Saivas* during *siṁhastha* (*kumbha melā*) congregation.
Śaiva sampradāya	Gosāin or Daśnāmī (Daśnāmī order includes — *Tīrtha*, *Āśram Vana*, *Araṇya*, *Giri*, *Parvat*, *Sāgar*, *Sarasvatī*, *Bhāratī* and *Purī*) saints.
Nāth sampradāya	
Nirmal sampradāya	
Udāsī sampradāya	*Baḍā* *Choṭā*
Dādu panth	

The various *akhāḍās* have been described below. Some of these have their centres in Ujjain.

Vaiṣṇava Akhāḍā

Name	Doctrine
Digambar	Tyāgī who has the universe as a garment.
Nirvāṇī	One who remains free from the attraction of belongings.
Nirmohī	One whom *moh* cannot touch.

Name	Doctrine
Khākī	One who remains engrossed in thinking about Brahmā.
Nirālambī	One who remains busy in propitiating his *iṣṭadeva.*
Santoṣī	One who has reached the stage of full satisfaction.
Mahānirvāṇī	One who believes that there is happiness in *nirvāṇa.*

Distribution of Akhāḍās to Sampradāyas

Sampradāya	*Akhāḍās*
Rāmānandi	Seven
Nimbārka	Seven
Mādhava	Two
Viṣṇu	Two
Nirvāṇī	Seven

The *niśāna* and position in *kumbha* procession of the *akhāḍās* are detailed below alongwith the mainstay of the philosophy of various *sampradāyas*.

Name of akhāḍā	*Niśāna*	*Position in kumbha procession*
Nirmohī (nine *akhāḍā*)	Silvery	First
Digambar (two *akhāḍā*)	*Pañcaraṅgī* (five colours)	Second
Nirvāṇī (seven *akhāḍā*)	Yellow	Last

Sampradāyas	*Philosophy*
Mādhava	*Dvaitavāda*
Nimbārka	*Dvaitādvaitavāda*
Rāmānujī	*Viśiṣṭādvaitavāda*
Viṣṇu	*Śuddhādvaitavāda*

The identification mark for the members of different *akhāḍā*s and *sampradāya*s lies in the variation of the *tilak*. As a whole, the Vaiṣṇavites apply a vertical *tilak* on the forehead. This again varies according to the *sampradāya* or *akhāḍā*. Each *sampradāya*, has several temples under its control. Of these Vallabha and Rāmānujī *sampradāyas* are very important in Ujjain. The former group has a *baiṭhaka* (place of meditation) adjacent to Sāndīpanī *āśram* in Ujjain. This is one of the eighty-four *baiṭhaka*s in India. So Ujjain is an important centre for this *sampradāya*. Rāmānujī *sampradāya* has a temple near Rāmghāṭ which has a *gopuram*. This is one of the identity marks for them. They run *Vedaśālā* for the students of the *maṭh*. The chief among the *Vaiṣṇava akhāḍās* is *Digambar akhāḍā*, which is located in Aṅkpaṭ area. The *bairāgī* saints camp here during *siṁhastha* (*kumbha melā*). *Tilak* mark and *iṣṭadeva* are the features by which the members can be identified. *Tulsimālā* is worn round the neck by all the *bairāgī* saints.

There is another group known as a *parṇāmī* who claim to be a *Vaiṣṇava sampradāya*. They worship only the headgear of Lord Śrī Kṛṣṇa, and they are not recognised by other *Vaiṣṇava sampradāyas*.

Besides, there is a small centre of Rādhā *sampradāya* which has Rādhā, the divine lover of Śrī Kṛṣṇa as *iṣṭadevī*. It is recognised by all the other *sampradāya*s. In any congregation of the *Vaiṣṇava*s the members of this *sampradāya* are invited with full honour.

Śaiva Sampradāya

Śaiva sampradāyas are predominant in Ujjain as it is the place of Lord Mahākāleśvar. They are identified with horizontal *tilak* marks on the forehead and garlands of *rudrākṣa*. The *akhāḍās* differ in their *iṣṭadeva, niśāna* and position in the *kūmbha* procession. The monastic formalities was introduced to the Śaivites by Ādi Śaṅkarācārya, perhaps under the influence of Buddhist organisations. Ādi Śaṅkarācārya travelled all over the country, met the teachers of various philosophies having followers on a regional basis and had discourses on the doctrines. He propagated his *advaita* philosophy and organised the scattered groups which had more differences than similarities. He also met Bhaṭṭa Bhāskar (of Avantikā) and Maṇḍana Miśra (Māhiṣmatī) of Mālwā. The latter accepted the supremacy of his thoughts. As part of his monastic approach, Ādi Śaṅkarācārya established four *maṭhas* (which are famous as Śaṅkara *maṭhas*) in four corners of the country — Dwārkā in the west, Govardhan in the east, Badrikāśaram in the north and Śṛṅgerī in the south. Each *maṭha* had a fairly distinct area of activities. In addition to the four *maṭhas*, he established a Kāmkoṭi Piṭha at Kāñcī. He had five *liṅgas* installed — Bhogaliṅga at Śṛṅgerī, Mokṣaliṅga at Cidambara, Muktiliṅga at Kedāreśvar, Bīrliṅga at Nepal and Yogaliṅga at Kāmehī. He popularised the *pūjan* of *pañcadevatā* (Śiva, Viṣṇu, Śakti, Sūrya and Gaṇapati) and appointed *Yajurvedī* Śrī Sureśvarācārya at Śṛṅgerī, *Sāmvedī* Hastīmalkācārya at Śārdā, *Ṛgvedī* Padmapad at Govardhana and *Atharvavedī* Ṭoṭakācārya at Jotirmaṭh as *ācāryas*. He has given details about the organisation of *maṭhas* in his *maṭhāmnāya*. There are several *upamaṭhas* apart from the four principal *maṭhas*.

According to *maṭhāmnāya*, there are seven *āgneya akhāḍās* and fifty-two *maḍīs*. There are eight *devas* in these *akhāḍās*. The existing *akhāḍās* are as follows:

Name	*Position in kumbha Procession*	*Īṣṭadeva*
Mahānirvāṇī	First	Kapildeva
Niranjanī	Second	Kārttikeya
Junā	Third	Dattātreya
Atal	With *Nirvāṇī*	Gaṇapati
Āvāhan	With *Niranjanī*	Dattātreya and Gajānan
Agni	Fourth	Agni
Ānanda	Fifth	Sūrya

The positions given above are unalterable. The *Nirvāṇī akhāḍā* here is at the temple of Lord Mahākāleśvar. Those belonging to the *Nirvāṇī akhāḍā* claim that previously the temple was under their control. The head office of *Nirvāṇī akhāḍā* is at Kankhal (near Haridvār) in Uttar Pradesh and of *Niranjani akhāḍā* at Allahabad. Other *akhāḍās* have their head offices at Kāśī. At Ujjain there are branches of *Nirvāṇī*, *Niranjani* and *Junā akhāḍā*. *Dattātreya akhāḍā* of Ujjain belongs to *Junā akhāḍā*. This is the main *akhāḍā* of the Gosāins here. The Daśnāmi ascetics camp here during the *kumbha melā* and take a holy dip at the *ghāṭs*. *Dattātreya akhāḍā* is situated on the opposite bank of Rāmghāṭ. *Bairāgi* saints take the holy dip on the Rāmghāṭ side. Ādi Śaṅkara also organised the Daśnāmī saints into ten groups — *Tīrtha, Āśram, Van, Araṇya, Giri, Parvat, Sāgar, Sarasvatī, Bhāratī*, and *Purī*. They are attached to the Śaṅkara *maṭhas*. Each of these Śaṅkara *maṭhas* has an independent philosophy, goddess and god. An ascetic gets the title assumed by his *guru* — that is, a *śiṣya* of a Purī teacher becomes Purī. The Daśnāmī group is the biggest *Śaiva sampradāya*.

Udāsī means one who does the *upāsanā* of Brahmā. There are two *akhāḍās* at Ujjain belonging to each of the two Udāsī groups, *baḍā* and *choṭā*. Udāsī ascetics get food and shelter at ordinary times but especially during *the kumbha melā* in the *akhāḍās*. There is a Udāsī *ghāṭ* in front of Udāsī *maṭha*. *Udāsī* saints bathe here during the *kumbha melā*. There is also a *Nirmal akhāḍā* here. Saints belonging to this *akhāḍā* and coming from distant branches camp here during *kumbha* congregation.

*Nāthpanthi*s predominate the Ujjain city as well as the surrounding rural areas. Their traditions assert that there were nine *Nāth*s and eighty-four *Siddha*s among the *Nāth* saints. Many temples are under the control of *virakta* or *gṛhasthī Nāth-yogi*s. Matsyendranāth was the founder of the sect, though Guru Gorakhnāth popularised it. It is believed that *yoga* was founded by Ādināth Bhagvān Śiva. So Śiva in a meditating posture is worshipped at *Nāth* centres. Three principles are mainly observed — purity of body, purity of mind and a controlled lifestyle. In all, there are twelve main centres of *Nāth sampradāya* in the sub-continent. A list has been given below:

Centre	*Founder*
Patal Bhubanesvar, Orissa	Satyanāth
Thinodhan, Kachh	Dharmanāth
Gorakhpur, Bihār	Śāntināth
Gorakhṭilā, Jhelum district	Lakṣmaṇanāth
Puṣkar, Rājasthān (*bairāgya panth*)	Bhartṛhari
Gaṅgāsar or Gaṅgāsāgar	Kapilnāth
Jodhpur, Rājasthān	Pabnāth
Dinājpur, Bengal	Aināth
Gurdāspur, Punjab	Gaṅgānāth

Centre	*Founder*
Ambālā, Punjab	Dhvajnāth
Near Indraprastha	Pagalnāth
Rāwalpiṇḍī	Nāgnāth

The *Nāth* saints claim that their centres are in good condition and that the Paśupatināth temple of Nepal belonged to them. The Gurkhā name for the Nepalese has been derived from the followers of Gorakhnāth. However, in Ujjain the Bhartṛhari cave is the main centre of the *Nāth sampradāya*. The *mahant* of this centre is the head of the *Nāth*s here. *Nāth-yogī*s camp here during the *kumbha melā*. They can be identified by their heavy *kuṇḍalas* (earrings), bunch of black (seven) threads around the neck, and the *śiṅga*. Among the *Nāthpanthī*s, Pūraṇa Bhagat, Gopicand and Bhartṛhari are popular in parts of the country. There are a number of *māch* dramas based on these characters which are staged by the various *māch* groups.

There are *Aghorpanthī*s or *Aughaḍapaṅthī*s at Ujjain who do not abide by any rules. They are very few and there is no organised unit here. This is also true of the *Kāpālika* sect. Though there is a temple of this sect there is no organised establishment.

Besides these *sampradāya*s and *akhāḍā*s of the old tradition which have a pan-Indian network, there are a few other religious organisations of different philosophies which do not belong to any *akhāḍā* and function independently. *Akhaṇḍa āśram* is one such organisation which has its headquarters at Citrakūṭa. They have centres at other places as well and call themselves Lord Śiva. But they accept the supremacy of the Śaṅkarācāryas also. Their centre here is well-organised and they run a dispensary providing treatment and medicine free of charge. Some contemporary saints of wide popularity have also established their centres in Ujjain. There is a centre run by Maharṣi Maheśa

Yogī which stresses on lessons in *yogas* and self-employment programmes for residents or inmates who live there. They have purchased a plot of land for the purpose and constructed a big building for the centre.

Traditionally, Ujjain has been the centre of astronomical studies. It was considered as the meridian by ancient Indian astronomers and it is said that the name of the *jyotirliṅga* Mahākāl is derived from this. It is the symbolic manifestation of a great time. The site of the temple is the real point from which the calculations were made. The temple was constructed as a precaution for not disturbing the site. Till date, this tradition of astronomical studies is alive. In appreciation of this tradition, Mahārājā Jaisingh of Jaipur constructed an observatory based on the model of those at Delhi, Jaipur and Varanasi. All these were constructed to help the local group of astronomers. At that time, he was the governor of Mālwā. The observatory is located on the bank of Śiprā on the southern outskirts. This is now under the supervision of the state meteorological department. Religiosity has been attached to astronomy in Ujjain since the early days. Two almanacs are published from Ujjain giving details of the position of the solar constellations.

4

The Abode of Lord Mahākāleśvar

I

UJJAIN or Avantikā is also known as *Mahākāl kī Nagarī* or City of Lord Mahākāl. Lord Mahakal is represented in *linga* form and is one of the twelve *jyotirlingas* (self-effulgent) of India. The number of *lingas* in Ujjain is uncountable. The Mahākāl *linga* is *svayambhū*, that is, nobody has installed it. It has such an influence on the people here that some use 'Mahākāl' as their surnames while some greet each other by saying *jai mahākāl.*

Lord Mahākāleśvar is said to have defeated and killed demon Tripurī in Ujjain and renamed it as Ujjayini or the place of triumph. Mahākāl is the *kālon-kā-kāl* (death of deaths) or that which has survived the effects of age. He is imperishable, indestructible, that which has no beginning or end (*anādi-ananta*). He has won over the lord of death and rules him. It is said that the Mahākāl temple was used as the meridian from which astronomical calculations were made in ancient India.

We find mention of Lord Mahākāl in various *Purāṇas* (*Linga Purāṇa, Skanda Purāṇa, Śiva Purāṇa*) and other religious texts. The area around Mahākāl went by the name of Mahākālvana, which suggests that it was a forest area. The legendary poet, Kālidāsa, has also mentioned Lord Mahākāl in his writings (*Meġhadūta*). It is believed that Lord Mahākāl is one of the three most sacred *liṅgas* and it is the only one in *mṛtyuloka* (earth). Of the remaining two, one is *Tārakaliṅgam* in the sky and the other, *Hata-kesaram* is in *pātāl*. Of the two *jyotirliṅgas* — Mahākāleśvar and Oṁkāreśvar — in Mālwa, the former is more important as after *kumbha snān* people have *darśana* of Lord Mahākāleśvar. The Mahākāl priests are respected among the brāhmaṇas and enjoy a special status. Some of the *pujārīs* give more importance to their attachment to Mahākāl than their individual standing or qualifications.

About the installation of Lord Mahākāl and construction of the temple, it is said that the *liṅga* is *svayambhū* and the temple has been constructed by Viśvakarmā, the divine architect. It was extended, enriched and enlarged during the reign of King Vikramāditya who hailed from the Mālavā dynasty. The period was marked by the construction of various temples. A golden image of King Vikrama was also installed as far as the saying goes. A huge bell used to hang from a golden chain and the temple walls were studded with gems. During the reigns of the Parmāra rulers, the temple was renovated and reconstructed. There was a boon in the construction of Śiva temples in Ujjain and the countryside under royal patronage. A particular pattern is assigned (the level of the *sanctum-sanctorum* is lower than the surface level). At some places the temples have been constructed at a higher level to give this form to the *garbhagṛha*. The *liṅga* is of moderate size, and has a good finish. Those of the Gupta period are larger and have a rough surface.

In the year 1235, Iltutmish, the Sultān of Delhi of the Slave dynasty massacred the city and pulled down the temple. Being fascinated by gems, he also damaged the *liṅga*. This was uprooted from the *jaladhārī* and thrown into the sacred Koṭitīrtha *kuṇḍa*. He took away the golden idol of Vikramāditya and other valuables to Delhi. The whole temple was destroyed and an *idgāh* was constructed at the site which was called Kāliāpīr. He also destroyed several other temples of the holy city.

During the following years, Mālwā changed hands several times, but mainly remained under Muslim rule. There were repeated attacks by Muslim invaders and the temples suffered dearly in those attempts. But some of the small temples survived these destructive ventures. In the vicinity of Mahākāl, a subsidiary temple of Mahākāl was constructed by the devotees. Actually a group of Śiva temples was constructed and this was to conceal the identity of the original idol. Possibly this was to save it from destruction.

There was no Mahākāleśvar temple for about five hundred years. The Marāṭhā power got established in Mālwā in the late eighteenth century. During the Muslim attacks, the Paramāras were pushed down to the deep Deccan area. Some are of the view that the survivors of the Paramāras became powerful and came to be known as Marāṭhās. There is not much support or foundation for this theory. Ujjain came under the possession of Rāṇojī Scindia, who was one of the most powerful *sardār*s in the Marāṭhā army. He made Ujjain his capital city and Mālwā became a part of the Marāṭhā confederacy under the leadership of Peśavā. Rāṇojī mostly remained busy in fighting wars for the Peśavā at various fronts. Particularly after the defeat at the Third Battle of Pānipat, the local chiefs tried to overcome the Marāṭhā supremacy. So the Marāṭhā chiefs were busy suppressing the revolts. Rāṇojī's *dewān*, Rāmcandra actually looked after the administration and was more popularly known as Rāmcandrabābā. He was informed about the existence of the ancient Mahākāl temple in the city. Under his leadership, a frantic search was made to find out the exact location and the *Śivaliṅga*. The local Brāhmaṇa groups supplied the information and based on this, the Koṭitīrtha *kuṇḍa* which was then filled with rubble and garbage was cleaned. The *kuṇḍa* was found and finally the sacred *liṅga* and the original *jaladhārī* were also found. Then the temple was constructed and the *liṅga* was installed. The present temple dates back to Marāṭhā rule. Afterwards several temples have come up in the area and have given it the form of a complex. The whole area covered by it is around ten acres of land.

The Mahākāl complex is in the southern part of the city and is about three kilometres from the railway station and the central bus stand. From Chatrī Cowk, the central thoroughfare, it is about a kilometre. In Ujjain, mini-buses, city buses, tempos, rickshaws and auto-rickshaws are the main means of public transport. Some of the mini-buses ply between Mahākāl temple and Freeganj railway station. Besides, one can avail oneself of other means including *tāṅgās* which are quite cheap. The area is known as 'Koṭ Mahallā' or the walled sector. Previously there was a boundary wall, the ruins of which still exist. It is said that there were several gates in this boundary wall but now only one exists. This is known as Caubīs Khambā. The gate stands on twenty-four big pillars. On the two sides there are two images of female deities who are worshipped during the *Navarātra* festival. Daily worship is also performed.

The Mahākāl complex stands on the east bank of Rudra Sāgar lake. From the back of the temple complex, a road leads to Rāmghāṭ via Harsiddhi Devī temple. The nearby *mahallā* is mainly populated by brāhmaṇas of various groups. There is no area of untouchables nearby. The temple is open to all the devotees and no distinctions are made on caste or creed. From the temple gate the straight road leads to the railway station. Enroute there is a market of shops selling flowers and other materials necessary for worship. The complex is at a higher mound. From the tonga stand near the gate the steps lead to the courtyard below. The huge gate stands over the steps. Beggars can be found sitting on their either sides. And there are shops selling flowers, coconuts and other materials necessary for making offerings.

II

The complex can be divided into three sectors — Koṭitīrtha Kuṇḍa area, Junā Mahākāl area and courtyard area. On the eastern part is the huge gate which is the main entrance. On the northern side there are two small gates, one each on the western and southern boundary walls. The whole courtyard and the complex is about fifteen feet lower than the level of the road. From the road spacious (ten feet wide) steps lead down to the base of the gate and then to the courtyard. On the southern, eastern and northern side of the courtyard is the old *dharmaśālā* divided into several sections for various purposes. The roof of these is at the road level. Railings have been fitted for safety purposes and they provide a good view of the courtyard during festivals. On the left side of the steps is a small temple of Gaṇapati. There are small shops which sell coconuts, etc. for *pūjan*. On the right is the composite stand for *tāṅgās*, auto-rickshaws, cycles and the parking area. From the steps to the road the beggars sit in two rows. There are flag poles fitted to the balcony over the *dharmaśālā* on the eastern and southern wings. The new *dharmaśālā* has been constructed over the north wing of the old *dharmaśālā* and it opens onto the road. There is a drinking water tap on the right side of the steps.

At the second landing of the steps leading to the courtyard stands the big gate. At the base of the gate on the left is the counter for selling *prasād* and tickets of various denominations depending on the type of *pūjan* one wishes to perform. On production of this ticket the recognised *paṇḍā* performs the *pūjan*. On the right is the shoe stand. Shoes should not be taken inside the courtyard. Some, however, take their shoes inside and keep them near their particular *paṇḍā*. The gate is at the middle of the eastern wing and divides the *dharamśālā* into two equal halves. Each wing is divided into several *casmās* (sections) and the arches show Muslim influence. On the left wing, behind the counter, is the camp of the home guard stationed for the temple. Next to this is the free *piāo* (water hut) for drinking water run by a Sindhī trader. On the right wing behind the shoe-stand there are two shops. They mainly trade in stone images of Mahākāl and other gods and goddesses of Ujjain, *rudrākṣamālā, tulasīmālā, yantras* and other things of worship which the pilgrims sometimes carry back as mementos. Next to them is a sacred institute, *Ravi-Veda-Dhāma,* which runs a *Veda-Pāṭhaśālā* for children. It has an office and quarters for the resident incharge. The institute has branches at Mahidpur and some other places in Mālwā. Its classrooms extend to the north wing of the *dharmaśālā*. In the northern wing next to the *pāṭhaśālā* is Lord Narasiṁha's temple. There are images of Lord Narasiṁha in the process of killing the demon Hiraṇyakaśipu, images of his consort, goddess Lakṣmī as well as of *bhakta* Prahlāda. All of these are in black stone. The temple has wooden fencing and a door to close it. Next to this small temple is a part of the armed police camp. After this is the passage leading to the northern gate which opens into the Harsiddhi road. On the west side of the passage, there is a raised platform on which there are two *Śivaliṅgas* in the name of Maṅgalnāth and Siddhanāth, and Ciṅtāharaṇa Gaṇapati's image. This Gaṇapati is one of the six sacred Vināyakas of Ujjain. After the passage is the armed police camp. Next to this camp is the temple of Viṭṭhal-Paṇḍharīnāth. The temple is dedicated to Lord Viṭṭhal-Rukma (the divine couple of Paṇḍharipur of Mahārāṣṭra).

Next to the *piāo* (in the east wing of the *dharmaśālā*) is the southern wing of the *dharmaśālā*. On its eastern end there are two rooms used by the *pujārīs* for keeping their belongings. This space is also used to store broken items. Next to this is the *Mahānirvāṇī akhāḍā* and the *gaddī* of the *mahant* for this *akhāḍā* in Ujjain. Next to it is the office of the Mahākāl Samiti, and next to that, the official residence of the watchman; the store for *bhog* material and *pūjan sāmagrī* (things necessary for the worship of Lord Mahākāl) and the kitchen for preparation of *bhog* (cooked food intended as offerings.)

The Mahākāleśvar temple stands with all its grandeur at the centre of the western part of the courtyard and it faces east. The main gate faces the temple and from the main gate there is a pathway to the temple gate at the end of the courtyard. In front of this gate there is a pool of water (six feet long and three feet wide) for washing the feet. To its right is the small temple of Bṛhaspateśvar Mahādeva. It has no doors and faces east. From the gate there are steps which descend to the *dālān* or *sabhāmaṇḍapa* on the east bank of the Koṭitīrtha *kuṇḍa*. Behind Bṛhaspateśvar Mahādeva temple, there is a staircase for going to the roof of the *dālān*. Between Bṛhaspateśvar temple and the north wing of the *dharmaśālā* is the temple of Swapneśvar Mahādeva. This is one of the eighty-four sacred *liṅga*s of Ujjain. It faces east and consists of a *garbhagṛha* and a *sabhāgṛha*. The *sabhāgṛha* has an enclosure and the Nandī there faces the *liṅga*. Inside the *garbhagṛha*, there is an image of Lord Gaṇapati on the left wall, goddess Pārvatī on the facing wall and Kārtik Svāmī on the right wall. The *jaladhārī* of the *liṅga* is directed towards the north. The temple dome has *kalaśa* (rows of pots) and the construction is old.

Facing the Swapneśvar Mahadeva temple is the temple of Saṅkaṭmocana Siddha Hanumān. The temple faces west and is of a recent period. The temple has a *garbhagṛha* and a *sabhāgṛha*. On its south, a little closer to the main gate, is the small temple of Sākṣīgopāl, an incarnation of Lord Viṣṇu. There are images of Śrīkṛṣṇa, Balarāma and their consorts, Rādhā and Revatī. The temple faces west, the dome of which has a shade over it. This temple is on the north of the pathway. On the south of the pathway, there is a similar sized temple of Lord Siddha Gaṇeśa, which faces north and is situated at the south-east corner of the Mahākāl temple. Behind this and in front of the courtyard — *sabhāgṛha* (at ground level) of Mahākāl temple, there is a sacred banian tree. Here the ladies observe *Vaṭ-sāvitrī* festival. There are also two sacred *nīm* trees on either side of the pathway. On the left side, adjacent to the west gate of the courtyard, is the temple of *ekādaśa* (eleven) *liṅgeśvar*. These represent the eleven *jyotirliṅgas*, other than Lord Mahākāleśvar. Eleven *liṅgas* and six images of Umā-Maheśa (characteristic sculpture of Mālwā) are to be found here. There is no door to this temple and the roof is flat. It faces east. Behind this is the temple of Trivisthāpeśvar Mahādeva which faces west. It is also one of the eighty-four sacred *liṅgas* of Ujjain. The *śikhar* has rows of *kalaśa* and *mañjarīs*, and there are figurines of Pārvatī and Viṣṇu on the projection in the slopes of the tomb. The *garbhagṛha* is a little deep and the *liṅga* is in the centre of the floor. The *jaladhārī* is directed north and images of Pārvatī and Gaṇeśa are on the north and the east wall of the *garbhagṛha*. There is an *aṣṭakoṇa* (eight-angled) ceiling and some stone figurines on the upper beam of the door. This temple is double-storeyed. There is a *liṅga* in the upper chamber too and the chamber opens to the west on the roof of the *dālān*. The *paṇḍās* use this place for smoking or for rest. Only the *paṇḍās* or the many *pujārīs* use it and it is not open to the public. Next to this temple there is a stone inscription under a cenotaph.

The whole courtyard has marble flooring. On the south of the pathway there is a *yajñaśālā* used for performing *yajñas* or for religious discourses. It is a twenty-feet square, raised platform near the main gate. At its south-east corner is the sacred grove of *vatpīpal* and *nīm*. The three sacred plants being at this place, the place is considered the abode of the three supreme gods, Brahmā, Viṣṇu and Maheśa. Under this grove, there is a temple without a door dedicated to Lord Hanumān. To its west is the newly-constructed Navagraha temple. There was an old Navagraha temple to the south of the Mahākāl temple. It was in a dilapidated condition and was removed in the year 1980 for the construction of the underground *sabhāgṛha*. The present Navagraha temple is open on four sides with a dome on four pillars. The *gṛhas* have been represented in *liṅga* form in their characteristic colour and are arranged in three rows. There are nine *liṅgas* in all for the nine planets.

A little westward are the steps leading to the newly-constructed underground *sabhāmaṇḍapa*. The steps descend and there are five domes on pillars to make the *sabhāmaṇḍapa* airy during a heavy rush. There are a number of benches fixed at various places in the courtyard for visitors. Next to the *sabhāmaṇḍapa* there is the temple of Nīlakaṇṭheśvar Mahādeva which faces east. It is at a height of about three feet from the ground level. The *śikhar* has the figures of Lord Brahmā and Maheśa. The Nandī is placed at the *sabhāgṛha* and in the *garbhagṛha*, which is at a lower level than the *sabhāgṛha*, there is the *liṅga* in the centre. Gaṇapati, Pārvatī and Kārtik Svāmī are on the south, west and north walls respectively. Attached to the main *garbhagṛha* is an enclosed place where there is a *Śivaliṅga*.

Behind this is a raised platform where two images of Lord Gaṇapati were found during recent construction work. People make offerings to these images. The old steps leading to the Koṭitīrtha *sabhāmaṇḍapa* have been demolished during reconstruction. At the surface level, a small temple is dedicated to Lord Viṣṇu and Gaṇeśa. An image of Khaṇḍaveśvar is also there and it forms the Khaṇḍaveśvar temple.

On the west of Nīlakaṇṭheśvar Mahādeva temple, there is another Śiva temple dedicated to Govindeśvar Mahādeva. Both these temples are more or less of the same size. The temple faces east with a small *sabhāmaṇḍapa* and a *garbhagṛha* and there is a Gaṇapati image in the upper door frame. This is like any other Śiva temple : the *garbhagṛha* in which there is the *Śivaliṅga* is at a lower level and the *jaladhārī* is towards the north. Gaṇapati, Pārvatī, Kārtik Svāmī are at their usual places (i.e. front door, left wall, facing wall). The Nandī in this temple is on the outlet of the Jaladhārī. The temple is in good condition. On the north of the temple there are steps leading down to the south bank of the Koṭitīrtha *kuṇḍa*. Between this temple and the kitchen for cooking *bhog* is a pathway that bifurcates : one path leads to the Junā Mahākāl area, while the other goes to the west side gate towards the Rudra Sāgar lake.

In the Junā Mahākāl area there are as many as twenty-one small and big temples. All the temples being in a dilapidated state, they were renovated before the 1980 *kumbha melā.* The biggest temple of this area is the Junā Mahākāl or older Mahākāl. It is said that under Muslim rule, in the absence of the original Mahākāl temple, devotees made offerings at this temple. In size, this is next to the main Mahākāl temple. It is also the only temple under private ownership.

The Anādikalpeśvar Mahādeva temple of Ujjain has one of the eighty-four *liṅga*s. In size it is the third largest temple in the whole complex. It has three sections — *garbhagṛha*, a spacious *sabhāgṛha* and a raised platform for the Nandī. The *garbhagṛha* is at a lower level than the surface and there is a huge *liṅga* at the centre of the *garbhagṛha.* An *abhiṣekpātra* hangs from the ceiling and there is a Gaṇapati image on the upper beam of the door. On the two sides of the door, there were paintings which have been spoiled due to repeated coats of whitewash. A painting depicts a Bhairava with a dog and above the doorframe, a panel shows the *rāsayātrā.* The sides of the door also have shelves for keeping idols. Inside the *garbhagṛha*, there are Gaṇapati, Pārvatī and Kārtik Svāmī on the south, west and north wall shelves respectively. The *jaladhārī* directs north and opens through a *magar* (alligator) face. The temple faces east. In the ceiling of the *sabhāmaṇḍapa* there are figures showing the *rāsayātra.* These figures, again, have been spoiled.

Behind this temple is the composite temple of Saptarṣi. All the temples are continuous and identical, and face the east. They are dedicated to seven saints and Arundhatī. In one temple, Kāśyap and Dhruva have been depicted in *liṅga* form. Four temples are dedicated to a saint each. The saints have also been represented in *liṅga* form. In the sixth temple, there is Vasiṣṭha and Arundhatī. All the venerated *ṛṣi*s and Arundhatī have been represented in *liṅga* form. None of these temples have a *sabhāgṛha.* A small garden has been developed and maintained by the *pujārīs*.

On the south of Anādikalpeśvar temple, there are three small Śiva temples. Two have side walls and a flat roof and the third one has only the roof resting on four pillars. Facing these there are two slightly bigger Śiva temples facing west. Next to these is the temple of Oṁkāreśvar Mahādeva which also faces east and has a *sabhāgṛha* and *garbhagṛhas*. To its right is a small Śiva temple in front of which the *kalpavṛkṣa* is inscribed on a stone plate. On the east of this temple is the twin temple of Lord Śiva and Govardhananāth. The *sabhāmaṇḍapa* of the Śiva temple is linked to that of the Govardhananāth temple. In the latter temple, there are images of Govardhana and Sarasvatīdevī. The Śiva temple is known as Govindeśvar Mahādeva. Adjacent to this temple is the temple of Vīr Hanumān, which is in good condition. The deity is in a standing posture facing south.

Besides, there are a couple of small Śiva temples of minor importance. These have been renovated during the last *kumbha melā* (1980). Of these Manakāmeśvar, Rameśvar and Kāśī-Viśvanātha are of moderate size and are important. The manakāmeśvar temple faces west and the *jaladhārī* in this temple is directed towards the east. It has a small *sabhāgṛha.* The *śikhar* is of lotus design with two constrictions. Rameśvar temple *śikhar* also has a lotus design. It is like any other Siva temple. The temple of Kāśī-Viśvanātha faces east and its jaladhārī is directed in the same direction. The roof of the *sabhāgṛha* is elliptical.

Junā Mahākāl or Vṛddha Kāleśvar temple is located in the southern corner of the complex. There is a small door in the southern boundary wall. It faces west and is divided into three parts. There is a *garbhagṛha*, a *sabhāgṛha* and a raised platform on which the Nandī presides. The level of the *garbhagṛha* is lower than the *sabhāgṛha*. The large-sized *liṅga* is at the centre of the *garbhagṛha* and *the abhiṣekpātra* hangs from the ceiling. There are Gaṇapati, Pārvatī and Kārtik Svāmī images on the upper beams of the door and walls. The *sabhāgṛha* is spacious with a *yajña kuṇḍa*. Here too, the *jaladhārī* directs north. There is a door at the entry of the *sabhagṛha* and the *pujāris* stay inside. The temple has a height of about sixty feet and there are rows of *kalaśa* in the temple *śikhar*. Behind this temple is the Rudra Sāgar lake.

Since the government took over the main Mahākāl temple, the Junā Mahakāl temple has become an important commercial centre and a place of earning for the traditional *paṇḍās*, who perform the rituals for their *jajmāns* here. The temple seems to date back to the Muslim period when the main Mahākāl temple was in ruins. The priests might have constructed it as a substitute for the Śiva worshippers and this was renovated and reconstructed during the early Marāṭhā rule. This is the leading temple of this section of the Mahākāl complex. In front of this temple there are *samādhis* of the deceased *mahants* of the Mahānirvāṇi *akhāḍā* and on each *samādhi* (memorial) there is a *liṅga*, the symbolical representation of the dead *mahants*.

Koṭitīrtha is the sacred tank with four wells on its four corners. Here people wash their hands and feet. Now washing of feet has been prohibited, and a small ditch has been made near the gate for the purpose. Koṭitīrtha is a very sacred tank. It is a square pond, the water level of which varies with the season. A story tells us that during the *Aśvamedha yajña*, Lord Rāma asked Hanumān to bring sacred water from all the *tīrthas*. After collecting water from various *tīrthas* (one crore in number) in a pot, Hanumān was returning to Ayodhyā. At Ujjain, however, he stopped for a while to worship Lord Mahākāl. Lord Mahākāl blessed Hanumān and asked him to pour some water into the *kuṇḍa* from his pot. Hanumān did so. The tank is said to contain the water of one crore *tīrthas*. Hence the name 'Koṭitīrtha'.

The *dālān* or a *sabhāmaṇḍapa* of Mahākāl is on its east bank and on the west bank is the Sanskrit College. Dewās *dharmaśālā* is on the south bank and is under the *pujārīs*. Its first floor has several small rooms which are used by the *pujārīs* to keep their things and to rest. Half of the first floor is the *dharmaśālā* and the remaining half is the residence of Śrī Lakṣmīnārāyaṇa Vyās, the *ācārya* among the *pujārīs*. There is a temple in this floor dedicated to the divine couple Lakṣmi-Nārayaṇa. On the north bank there are two temples, one of Lord Śiva and the other dedicated to Lord Gaṇapati. These have been renovated during the last *kumbha melā*. Behind these is the residence of the late Paṇḍit Sūryanārāyaṇa Vyās. On the north-west corner of the tank there is a gate opening into the Harsiddhi road. The devotees coming from the Śiprā *ghāṭ* after a bath during festivals enter the temple area through this gate. At the centre of the *kuṇḍa* there is a criss-cross, trident-shaped fountain with five projections. This fountain is one of the additions made to the *kuṇḍa* during the last *kumbha* (*siṁhastha*) *melā*.

From all directions, steps descend to the water intercepted by landings. There are a number of *liṅgas*, some with roof only or even open. On the eastern bank, there is Lord Śani in *liṅga* form which is the first *liṅga* from the north side. Then there is the temple of Hanumānjī on a platform facing (Dās Hanumān) Rāma-Sītā Mandir of the *dālān*. Next to the steps from the *dālān* are two temples — one of Rāmeśvar Mahādeva and the other of Koṭeśvar Mahādeva (or lord of Koṭitīrtha). Both are in *liṅga* form and are important *liṅgas* in the Mahākāl area. They are worshipped before the performance of some *pūjās* for Lord Mahākāleśvar. Then, there are steps from the *dālān* that have four Śiva temples with a flat roof and of a similar size next to them.

On the south bank there are many temples. The first one is a *Śivaliṅga*, with a Gaṇapati image in a niche. Next to it is the temple of Sūryamukhī Hanumān. It is a temple facing east and hence the name Sūryamukhī Hanumān. Behind this is the idol (head) of the legendary King Vikramāditya. Next to this is the image of Lord Sūrya mounted on a chariot pulled by seven horses. Then there are seven *liṅgas* with a roof and three *liṅgas* in the open and the image of Lord Kūrma, all in a row.

The temple of the western bank starts with two *Śivaliṅgas* with a roof from the south side. Next to it is the image of Bikal Bhairava, which is also known as Gorā Bhairava. After this is a composite temple with five lotus-designed tombs known as the Cālīs Liṅgeśvar temple. There are forty *liṅgas* which represent the stars and forty-four other *liṅgas*. In Ujjain people perform *yātrā* of the *caurāsī liṅga* (visiting and worshipping of eighty-four sacred *liṅgas* of Ujjain). One can also make offerings to Caurāsī Liṅgeśvar and avoid visiting all the eighty-four Liṅgas in a *yātrā*. To the north of this temple there are three *Śivaliṅgas* having roof. The second one is that of Indreśvar Mahādeva. Lord Indra has been represented in *liṅga* form. The chamber which bears the *liṅga* is filled with water and the *liṅga* is worshipped to get relief from drought and ensure good rains.

The north bank has also a number of *liṅgas*. The westernmost *liṅga* has four faces and is known as Paśupatināth. Then there are two *Śivaliṅgas* with roof. Next to this is the *pañca liṅgī* Mahādeva (five *liṅgas* in a Jaladhārī). After this there is a Jaladhārī in which the Nandī is in a sitting posture with a *Śivaliṅga* on its back. This is followed by a row of four *liṅgas* with no roof. In all these cases the *jaladhārī* directs north and the water of Koṭitīrtha *kuṇḍa* is offered to Lord Mahākāleśvar.

In the whole complex, the temple of Lord Mahākāleśvar is the most important and largest. The temple is five-storeyed and has five *sabhāmaṇḍapa* of different sizes at various levels. The largest one is the *dālān* on the bank of Koṭitīrtha to the west of the temple. Next in size is the underground *sabhāmaṇḍapa*, constructed during the 1980 *siṁhastha melā*. This is in the south of the temple. In the east there are three *sabhāmaṇḍapa*s — one at the surface level, the second above it and the third above the second. In size, the one at the surface level is the largest and the topmost, the smallest.

The gorgeous temple faces east and has a height of eighty-eight feet from the surface. Keeping pace with the Parmāra tradition, the *jyotirliṅga* is in the underground chamber. The newly-constructed underground *sabhāmaṇḍapa* is on its south side. There are skylights for ventilation in the underground chamber. One of them is fitted with an exhaust fan to suck out the warm air and the other opens into the *sabhāmaṇḍapa* in the courtyard. One can view Lord Mahākāl through this opening. In the surface level chamber (just above the *jyotirliṅga*) is Oṁkāreśvar in *liṅga* form. It is the replica of the *jyotirliṅga* at Oṁkāreśvar. At this level there is a *sabhāmaṇḍapa* in front of the Oṁkāreśvar *garbhagṛha*. There are three doors on the three other sides of the temple. The west side door is that of the *dhūnī* room. An *akhaṇḍa dhūnī* (uninterrupted sacred fire) is maintained in this room by burning dried cowdung cakes. The ash is used for *bhasmārati pūjan*. Previously, ash from the *śmaśān* was used for this purpose. The southern door leads to the narrow and steep stairs (two feet six inches wide) that lead to the upper floors. On the first floor there is no *liṅga* in the *garbhagṛha* (the chamber above the *liṅga* of Oṁkāreśvar). It is place of storage for the firewood and *kaṇḍā* (cowdung cakes) used for the sacred fire. In the space between the *garbhagṛha* and *sabhāgṛha* there are two images on the wall shelves — one of Lord Viṣṇu and the other of Lord Gaṇapati. The *sabhāgṛha* is partially covered. In the floor above is the image of Lord Nāgcandreśvar, which is on the wall where the stairs end. Nāg King Vāsukī spreads its hood over the divine couple of Umā-Maheśa. The *sabhāgṛha* has a partial roof. In the *garbhagṛha* there is a *Śivaliṅga*. It is believed that a *Śivaliṅga* is always installed over an important *Śivaliṅga* in the lower chamber so that one cannot walk directly over the *Śivaliṅga* below. The stairs end at the third floor where the speakers are fitted in four directions. From there one can come out on the *śikhar*. There are stone projections in the form of discontinuous stairs to reach the top of the temple. The *jhaṇḍā* (flag) is fitted on the top which is changed on specific occasions. The temples of Oṁkāreśvar and the *jyotirliṅga* are open to the visitors daily. The devotees can have *darśana* of Lord Nāg Candreśvar only once a year on the day of the *Nāg Pañcamī* festival.

The temple is made of stone blocks of different shapes and sizes. Up to the third floor there is no decoration on the temple wall. It is straight and smooth and the *śikhar* starts from the third floor. It has rows of *mañjarīs*, each with rows of *kalaśas* (pots) at seven levels. These seven levels are symbolic of seven *svargas*. The number of *mañjarīs* reduces with the height and they terminate in a single and big one. The number of *mañjarīs* in any row is of odd number as an odd number is considered more auspicious than an even number. In all, there are one hundred and twenty-one *mañjarīs* in the *śikhar*. The *śikhar* is like a cone on top of which is the *maṅgala kalaśa*. It is made of gold donated by the Scindias of Gwālior. Above this is fitted a mercury vapour light which is visible from a considerable distance. The *śikhar* is painted yellow which is an auspicious colour. The room on the northern side of the Oṁkāreśvar temple has remained closed for some time, following a dispute between the *pujārīs* and the Scindias.

From the gate at the west end of the courtyard near the Liṅgeśvar temple, steps descend to the *dālān* or the Koṭitīrtha side *sabhāmaṇḍapa*. This *sabhāmaṇḍapa* is about eighty feet long and fifteen feet wide. At the northern end, there is a bounded map of India showing the distribution of *jyotirliṅga* as well as the nearest township. There are also large photographs (five feet long and three feet wide) of all the *jyotirliṅgas* fitted to the upper portion of the *kuṇḍa* side wall and these have been fixed above the pillars. In each of these photographs the name and exact location of the *jyotirliṅgas* are given as a guidance. The first image on the northern end of the *dālān* is that of Avantidevī, who is believed to be the tutelary goddess of Avantikā. The Rāma-Jānakī temple is in the front and faces west. It has the marble images of Lord Rāma, Lakṣmaṇa and Sītā. In the long corridor of the *sabhāmaṇḍapa*, there are seventeen *takhtas* or seats for the *paṇḍās*, who have the hereditary right over them.

The staircase next to the Rāma-Jānakī temple has the temple of Candrādityeśvara next to it in the east wall. This is one of the eighty-four sacred *liṅgas* of Ujjain. The *liṅga* is inside the *garbhagṛha*. The temple faces west while the *jaladhārī* is towards the north. In front of this temple on the floor of the *sabhāmaṇḍapa* is a *liṅga*. Next to this is the *ābhūṣanakakṣa* (store for clothes, precious stones and ornaments of Lord Mahākāla) in the east wall. This is guarded by armed police round the clock. There is a metal mask of Lord Mahākāla and a big photograph showing Lord Rāma and Sītā worshipping Lord Mahākāla. After the *ābhūṣanakakṣa*, there is the image of Devī Annapūrṇa. The image being under a thick coat of oil and vermilion, its form cannot be made out. There is an image of Bhairava next to that of goddess Annapūrṇā. It is followed by the head of Bīrbhadra, an army commander of Lord Śiva. In the wall there are two shelves — one has a marble image of Gaṇapati, and the other also has a Gaṇapati image but under a thick coating of vermilion. The latter one is more important. From the marble-floored *sabhāmaṇḍapa* there are three passages leading to the underground chamber. In the first passage there is a silver-plated door with door panels of similar finish. In the centre of the upper beam, there is an image of Lord Gaṇapati. Above the door is a large photograph of Lord Gaṇapati killing a demon. From this gate there are steps leading to the underground corridor. Steps from the second passage meet the first one. These steps are only two feet six inches wide and are very old. Steps from the third or the last passage, which is at the southern end of the *sabhāgṛha*, are quite wide (five feet) and lead to the newly constructed *sabhāgṛha.* The first passage is normally used for entry. During a heavy rush, the first two passages are closed and the crowd is allowed through the new passage. The steps of the first passage lead to the older corridor. At a turning in the steps we find another Gaṇapati image in the wall. The corridor leads to the door of the underground chamber and goes beyond. From the east end of the corridor, steps go up to the gate opening into the courtyard near the *sabhāmaṇḍapa.* Where the underground chamber opens into the corridor, there is another gate which opens into the newly-constructed underground *sabhāmaṇḍapa.* This is made in such a way that people can have *darśana* of the *jyotirliṅga* from the newly-constructed *sabhāmaṇḍapa.* There are door shutters at this gate. In this *sabhāmaṇḍapa,* which is hexagonal in shape, there is the Nandī facing Mahākāla and a *dānapeṭī* (box for donations). The *sabhāmaṇḍapa* is twenty feet square and is quite airy due to the elevation of the central dome. At the southern end, there are spacious steps, leading up to the courtyard. On the south wall there is a coloured engraving showing the twelve months of the zodiac.

The third *sabhāmaṇḍapa* is on the eastern side of the courtyard in front of the Oṁkāreśvara temple. Here Lord Oṁkāreśvara, a big *liṅga,* is in the *garbhagṛha.* There are door shutters and a Gaṇapati image in the centre of the upper beam. Inside, on the south wall is Lord Gaṇapati, on the west wall the image of goddess Pārvatī and on the north wall, that of Kārtik Svāmī. The water-filled *abhiṣekpātra* hangs from the ceiling exactly over the sacred *liṅga.* The ceiling has an *aṣṭakoṇa* form.There is a space between the *sabhāgṛha* and *garbhagṛha.* At the end of it is the skylight, through which the Mahākāleśvara *liṅga* can be seen in the lower chamber. The passage is built in such a way that the first rays of the rising sun fall on the *jyotirliṅga* through this skylight. The Oṁkāreśvara and Nāgcandreśvara temples are under the control of the *Mahānirvaṇī akhāḍā*. The *sabhāmaṇḍapa* in front of Lord Oṁkāreśvara is hexagonal with fifty-five stone pillars. The outer pillars have engravings, differing from one another. These pillars are so arranged that from the easternmost end one can have *darśana* of Lord Oṁkāreśvara and one need not enter the temple. These pillars seem to be very old and they were used in the original temple of the Paramāra age. In the *sabhāmaṇḍapa*, there is the Nandī facing the *liṅga*. Above this is the fourth *sabhāgṛha* with twenty-eight stone pillars. It has a balcony and in the space in front of the store there are images of Viṣṇu and Umā-Maheśa. Lord Siva's marriage is also depicted here. Above this *sabhāmaṇḍapa* is the fifth *sabhāmaṇḍapa* in front of Lord Nāgcandreśvar Mahādeva with nine stone pillars. During *darśana* of Nāgcandreśvar (on *Nāg Pañcamī* day only) it becomes very crowded.

At the entry to the underground chamber from the corridor the door frame is silver-plated. The heavy, silver-plated door shutters seem to be very old. There are figures on the door shutters depicting the *pūjārinī* image. At the centre of the upper beam there is an image of Lord Gaṇapati. The floor of the chamber is laid with marble and is about ten feet square. In the west wall shelves there is a marble image of Lord Gaṇapati. Pārvatī is on the north wall and Kārtik Svāmī is on the east wall, both in white marble. The sacred *jyotirliṅga* is at the centre of the chamber. The *liṅga* is quite big and it is about two-and-a-half feet above the ground. The *jaladhārī* encircles it and it is directed towards the east here. Lord Mahākāl faces the south. From the end of *jaladhārī* there is a channel leading to the water storage section below the corridor. The extra water is taken out from this storage from time to time. The *jaladhārī* as well as the base of the *liṅga* is silver-plated. Devotees cannot cross the *jaladhārī* and so they take a half-round of Lord Mahākāl. There are snake engravings on the *jaladhārī*. The *abhiṣekpātra* hangs from the ceiling right above Lord Mahākāl and it remains filled with water, which drop on the *liṅga* through a pore at the base of the abhiṣekpatra. Near the end of the *jaladhārī*, there is the sacred *triśūla* (trident) implanted. Around the *jaladhārī* there is a railing six inches high. On the face of the *liṅga* (south side) there is a deep scar which is said to be a result of the damage done by Iltutmish, the Sultān of Delhi in the thirteenth century. There are two *nandadīpas* on the south side of the *jaladhārī*, one at the west and the other on the east, and an uninterrupted flame (light) is maintained in both of these. Some of the devotees bring *ghī* and pour this into the *dīpas* as part of their offerings. Each of these *dīpas* is six inches square in size and about one-and-a-half feet high. There are two wooden stools, the seat of the *pūjārīs* on the west of the *jaladhārī* and on the south of it. Behind one of the seats, a small cupboard is there for keeping items of worship.

There is a hole on the west wall believed to be the place of Bhūśūṇḍikāk (the crow sage), who attained salvation through Śiva-worship. There are two exhaust fans in the chamber and a pair of fluorescent tube lights are fitted to the ceiling. The ceiling has the shape of *aṣṭakoṇa* (eight-angled shape) with eight arms covered with glass. *Rudrāṣṭakas* are written on these arms. The ceiling on which the *Rudrayantra* is engraved is silver plated. In the *Rudrayantra*, sixty-four *ślokas* are engraved. Due to constant smoke from burning camphor, the colour has faded and so the *ślokas* cannot be read properly. There is a *dānapeṭī* by the side of the *jaladhārī* for the devotees to make offerings.

III

The Mahākāl temple attracts people from different walks of life throughout the day. *Pūjās* and other activities keep the area lively during the evenings. At almost every hour of the day there are ritual performances. The rituals can be grouped under three main categories — *nitya pūjan* or daily rituals, rituals performed during festivals round the year, special rituals including those specified for pilgrims.

The daily activities in the temple starts at about three in the morning. The *pujārīs* rinse their mouths, have a bath and then ring the bell (to wake up the Lord). A pot full of water from the *kuṇḍa* is used to perform the *Gaṇapati pūjan* and *ḍyoḍhī pūjan* (gate worship). The lock is opened with the loud uttering of *jai mahākāl.* Chanting of Mahākāl *ślokas* (couplets) starts with *namaskār* to Nandīgaṇa. It is followed by the *pūjan* of other *gaṇa* or the army chiefs of Lord Śiva such as Vīrabhadra, Nandī, Bhṛṇgī and Kīrtimūkha. This is followed by *Gaṇapati pūjan* and then the lock on the door of the Mahākāl chamber is opened. With the chanting of *Trayambakeśvarstuti* (prayers of Lord Trayambakeśvar), the *garbhagṛha* is thoroughly cleaned. After this, Gaṇapati, Pārvatī and Kārtik Svāmī in the wall shelves are worshipped. After cleaning the *liṅga* and *yoni* (*jaladhārī*) as well, Lord Mahākāleśvar is worshipped with *pañcāmṛt* (five items) and *ṣoḍaśopacāra* (sixteen items of worship). It is followed by *pūjan* of *dīpak* (light), Nāg (snake), Sūrya (sun), Candra (moon), and Pāñcadevatā or Pañcānan (Gaṇapati, Pārvatī, Kārtik Svāmī, Nandīgaṇa and Mahākāl) with *gandhākṣat* (*abīr, gūlāl, kumkum* and *sugandhī*). Though this is done by the official priest, others do not miss it as it is the main *pūjan.* After this *dhūpāratī, dīpak darśana* and *amṛtmātra naivedyam* (small amounts of sweets) are offered. This is followed by *karpūrāratī* (lighting of camphor) and offering *pūjā* by the special *bhaktas* (they are brāhmaṇas and mostly relatives of the *pujārīs, paṇḍās* or educated men who regularly attend this *pūjan* known as *bhasmāratī*). During this *pūjan,* brāhmaṇa *bhaktas* other than *pujārīs,* keep chanting Rudra (Vedic *ślokas*) continuously. Then the official *pujārī* performs *pūjan* with *gaṅgājala* (water of the sacred Ganges), *pañcāmṛt, naivedya, jaladhārā* (water show), *dūdhadhārā* (milk shower), as prescribed in the *Vedas,* i.e., Rudrābhiṣek, *ṣaḍaṅganyās* (purification of the whole body), *jaladhārā,* and *abhiṣeka* with *namak camak.* This is followed by Rudrābhiṣeka *śāntipāṭha* and *śṛṅgāra* (decoration). The *mahant* of the *Mahānirvāṇī ākhāḍā* puts sacred *bhasma* over the *liṅga*, which is his right. Lord Mahākāl is then decorated with *rudrākṣamālā* and *ābhūṣaṇa* (Nāg, headgear, candra, *muṇḍamālā*, *bilva pātra*, flowers). After this, *āratī pūjan* is performed which includes *āratī* of *pañcānan*, with *jhāñja*, *śaṅkha*, *ḍamru*, *ghaḍyāl* and *nagāḍā*. It takes about half an hour and only in this *pūjan* are *ḍamru* and *śaṅkha* played. This is followed by the concluding part of the *pūjan*, which includes *mantrapuṣpāñjali*, *saṅkalpa*, *bhajan* and *kīrtan* (devotional songs). This *pūjan* is known as *bhasmāratī pūjan* and is the most important. There are special morning bus services from neighbouring towns to reach Ujjain and to participate in this *pūjan*. Restrictions are imposed on the devotees to enter the chamber and make offerings till the *pūjan* is over. Ladies cannot enter the chamber. One has to take a bath early in the morning to attend it and stitched clothes cannot be worn. Only a *dhotī* can be worn, keeping the upper part of the body bare. Mostly the brāhmaṇas enter the chamber and the sacred thread is their identity — which will be visible due to the bare upper part of the body. Some non-brāhmaṇas are regular participants. Though there are no official restrictions, members of the scheduled castes do not attend. After *bhasmāratī*, the pouring of the water starts and it continues uninterruptedly till the afternoon *pūjan*. In case of *bhāt pūjan*, restrictions are imposed for half an hour or so.

Prātaḥkālīna pūjan is performed between 8:30 a.m. and 10:30 a.m. It consists of *pañcāmṛt pūjan*, *ṣoḍaśopacāra pūjan*, *nyās*, *dhyān*. *Mahā bhog* (curd and rice) and seasonal fruits are offered. This is followed by *madhyāhnakālīna pūjan*, which is performed at about 11:00 a.m. Besides *pañcāmṛt pūjan* (*dahī*, *dūdh*, honey, sugar and *gaṅgājala*), *antima snān* with sacred Gaṅgā water is also performed. The *pūjan* is done with *candan* (sandal) *akṣat*, flowers, *kumkum*, *bilva pātra*. *Ṣaṣṭa bhog* or food with six varieties of taste — *khaṭṭā*, *mīṭhā*, *turā*, *carkā*, *namkīn* and *ānūnā* — and *mahābhog* are offered. It is famous as *chappana pakvāna* (fifty-six items). The *ārati* concludes the offering. *Mahānirvaṇī akhāḍā* has the right over the things offered after *pūjan*.

At about five in the evening, the *sāyaṁkālīna pūjan* is performed. Before this, pouring of water is stopped for the day. Lord Śiva swallowed the venom secreted by Vāsukī, the King of Snakes (Nāg King) at the time of *samudra-manthan*. So Lord Śiva loves to have a water shower and pouring water is the best way of worshipping Lord Śiva. Before *sāyaṁkālīna pūjan*, the *garbhagṛha* is also thoroughly cleaned and the *abhiṣekpātra* is removed. Decorations are made on the *liṅga*. This means mainly giving a human face to the *liṅga*. People come in the evening especially to see the *śṛṅgār*. *Pujārī*s try to make the function as attractive as possible by their art work on the *liṅga*. Various types of decorations are made intermittently to avoid monotony. *Pūjan* consists of *nyās*, *dhyān*, *pañcāmṛta*, *pañcānan pūjan*, *rudrābhiṣeka* and *gaṅgājala snān*. After this, the public is allowed to enter the chamber for *darśana*.

Sandhyāratī pūjan is also important and attracts visitors. It is done at about 7:30 p.m. A member of the Bhoi caste rings the bell, announcing the time of the *ārati*. *Pūjan* is offered. A detailed *ārati* is the most important part of this *pūjan* which takes an hour to complete. Milk with *kesar*, *kastūrī*, *naivedya* of *khīr* and *mālpuā* are offered as *bhog*. Before the *ārati* the *maśālcī* comes with the *maśāla* (torch) and remains till the end. In this *ārati* cymbals are played. Till the end of the *ārati*, devotees are not allowed to enter and after the *ārati*, a *pujārī* takes the *ārati* (sacred flame) to the gathered devotees. The devotees put some coins as *dāna* while accepting the blessing of the *ārati*. The *dāna* goes to the *pujārī*.

At about eleven in the night the last *pūjan* or *śayanāratī* is performed with *abīra*, *gulāla*, *kumkum* and *itra*. *Pañcāmṛta* or water is not used and *bhog* consists of sweet meats. *Pūjan* is done with *campā* flower and *bilva patra*. *Ārati* is performed by burning camphor sticks and betel nut is offered. Lord Mahākāl is believed to rest after this and hence the temple is closed for the day.

Besides these *nitya pūjans*, there are special *pūjans* performed during festivals. The time of various *nitya pūjans* alters on such occasions. An account of the rituals round the year will give a complete idea about them. In Mālwā the *Vikram Samvat* is followed for the rituals and festivals. According to this, the month starts on a full moon day and ends by the next full moon day. By and large, the *Vikram Samvat* is followed in Ujjain. Ujjain was under Marāṭhā rule for a considerable period of time. The Marāṭhās followed the Śālivāhana *śaka* calendar, where the month starts on *amāvasyā* (dark) and ends on the next dark day. Thus, there remains a difference of a fortnight in the two calendars. Due to this, some festivals are repeated. Monday is a special day at the Mahākāl temple, as it is believed to be the birth day of Lord Śiva. There is rush of devotees for *darśana* in the temple. Some take a vow to eat a single principal meal or observe a partial fast on each Monday for satisfying some wish or for good fortune.

Guḍipāḍbā falls on the *Caitra pratipadā* day of the bright half. It is the new year day. On this date a procession is taken out from Siṁhapurī and Bhāksipura, the two brāhmaṇa-populated areas. This procession is taken out as *Ger*. Participants are mostly *pujārīs/paṇḍās* of the Mahākāl temple. In the month of *Baisākha, pañcakośī yātrā* is the important event besides the *kumbha melā*. In *kumbha melā*, on special dates, people take bath in Śiprā river and have *darśana* of Lord Mahākāl. *Pañcakośī yātrā* is to take a round of this *kṣetra*. It starts from Nāgcandreśvar Mahādeva temple in Paṭnibājār on the tenth day of the dark half in the *Caitra* month. After visiting the four *Dvārapāla* Śiva temples in four directions on foot, devotees come to the Rāmghāṭ. Some participate in *aṣṭatīrthī* (visiting twenty-eight *tīrthas*) *yātrā* along the course of the Śiprā. During this *yātrā*, they take a bath at every *tīrtha* and offer *pūjā*. Finally at the end, they take a bath and have a *darśana* of Lord Mahākāl. During such *yātrā*s there is a fixed route which marks the traditional boundary of Mahākālvana. *Akṣaya tṛtīyā* falls on the third day of the bright half and is considered as the most auspicious day to start any venture. People come here in large numbers to be blessed.

In the month of Jyeṣṭha *pradoṣa pūjan* is done at seven in the evening usually on the thirteenth or fourteenth day of both the dark and bright half. On the event of *pradoṣa* Lord Mahākāl observes a fast, and so there is no *bhog* offering in all the *pūjan*s during the day. In the evening after *pradoṣa pūjan*, *bhog* is offered. *Pradoṣa śani* and *soma pradoṣa* (*pradoṣa* falling on Saturday and Monday) are very important.

Caturdaśī (fourteenth day) of the dark half is observed specially in every month. Bhairava *pūjan* is done on the *Āsāḍhī pūnam* day which is also popularly known as Bhairava *pūnam* and is observed as *Gurupūnam* too at the Navagraha temple. Bṛhaspati, considered as the *guru* (teacher) of the gods, is worshipped. *Amāvasyā* on Monday and on Saturday have special significance and people take a bath at Rāmghāṭ and Triveṇī respectively. On such occasions there remains a good congregation of devotees coming mainly from neighbouring areas. Various castes and tribes have a *darśana* of Lord Mahākāl and visit the Mahākāl temple, and hence there is an extra rush of devotees. Extra rush means more earnings for the *pujārī*s and other brāhmaṇas offering sacred services. On the eleventh day of the bright half is the *Dev-soni-egāras* that marks the beginning of *Cāturmās* (sacred four months) which end with *Dev-uṭhni-egāras* on the eleventh day of the bright half in the month of *Kārtik*. During this period, marriages cannot be performed and religious persons stay put in a camp.

The month of *Śrāvaṇa* is the most important for Lord

Mahākāl. On every Monday, a Mahākāl *savārī* (procession) is taken out. It goes to the Rāmghāṭ and Gopāl Mandir and returns to the temple. For the completion of the trip, it takes several hours (3 to 4 hours). There were differences between the Mahārāṣṭrians and others based on the calendars about the observance on Mondays of the *Śrāvaṇa* month. A compromise has been reached whereby half of the *Śrāvaṇa* month is observed according to one of the two calendars (Vikram and Śālivāhana) and the other half, according to the other calendar. There are six *savārīs* in all. From third *savārī* onwards, the number of *jhāṅkīs* is increased. Lord Mahākāl is taken around. The procession starts from the temple in the afternoon and reaches Rāmghāṭ where *āratī* is performed to Mahākāl and the river Śiprā. From the other bank the *mahant* of Dattā *akhāḍā* performs *āratī* of Mahākāl. From Rāmghāṭ it goes to Gopāl Mandir where the main *pūjarī* of Gopāl Mandir makes offerings to Lord Mahākāl. Then it returns to the temple via Paṭnībājār. Offerings are made by people and temple priests of the temples en route (*Śaiva* and *Vaiṣṇava* temples, through mainly of the *Vaiṣṇava* type). Special police arrangements are made for the *savārī*.

On the fifth day of the bright half, the *Nāgpañcamī* festival is observed. Only on this occasion the temple of Nāgcandreśvara on the second floor is opened for the devotees to have a *darśana* and perform *pūjan*.The whole temple complex is illuminated and special arrangements are made to manage the huge crowd. The occasion attracts people equally from the rural and urban areas of Mālwā. Till late at night, devotees have *darśana*. A magistrate is stationed to maintain law and order and the collector and the sub-divisional officer supervise the arrangements. They do the same for the *savārī* and *pañckośī yātrā* too. The *Nāgpañcamī* festival of Mahākāl gets wide coverage from the press.

Śrāvaṇa pūnam day is observed as *Rakṣābandhana*. A sister ties the *kaccā dhāgā* (sacred protective thread) to the wrist of her brother, who will protect her in danger and help her in need. People here also offer *rākhī* to Lord Mahākāl and worship him for protecting them from evils and dangers. This is also observed as *śravaṇī* by the brāhmaṇas (Śuklā Yajurvedī), who change their sacred thread on this day by observing a ritual. The new sacred thread is also offered to Lord Mahākāl. A special attraction is the *bhāṇg-kā-śṛṅgār* of Lord Mahākāl in the evening. The sacred *liṅga* is covered with a thick layer of *bhāṅg* and a facial form is made with the help of *kiśamiśa* and cashew nuts. The following day, this is distributed as *prasād* and a major portion is consumed by the *pujārīs* and *paṇḍās*. It draws people in large numbers. *Śrāvaṇa* is an auspicious month for *abhiṣek* and *pūjan* of Lord Mahākāl.

Hartālikā tīja is observed on the third day of the bright half of *Bhādon*. Ladies go to the Saubhāgeśvar Mahādeva temple and also come to the Mahākāl temple to make offerings to Lord Mahākāl for the long life and welfare of their husbands. In the *Vaṭ sāvitrī* festival also, the ladies worship the sacred banian tree of the courtyard for the well-being of their husbands. They also have *darśana* of Lord Mahākāl.

From *Bhādon pūnam*, the *Śrāddhapakṣa* starts and continues till *Kuār amāvasyā*. People perform ancestral worship during this period. They perform this on a specific date (the *tithi* of expiry) and have a *darśana* of Lord Mahākāl. This fortnight is also observed as *Umāśāñjhī* festival. It is said that Umā, Śiva's wife, performed this festival to gain a good husband and got Lord Śiva as her husband. This is a festival observed by unmarried girls in search of good husbands. Every day new graphical designs are made on house walls and the designs are replaced the next day. At Mahākāl temple there is a five feet square marble plate. Beautiful designs are made on this plate with coloured powders by the *pujārīs* every day. The designs are altered daily and on the final day, the *pujārīs* try to make it most attractive. The people come to see the *śṛṅgāra*.

The *Daśaharā* festival is observed as *Vijaya Daśamī* and it is the festival of conquest. Lord Rāma defeated the demon king Rāvaṇa on this day. It is also observed at the Mahākāl temple. The *sāyaṁkālina pūjan* is done at 3 p.m. and the pouring of water is stopped. The *liṅga* is covered with a metal mask. After worshipping the mobile image of Lord Mahākāleśvar, it is taken out in procession to the *Daśaharā maidān*, which is at the other end of the city. *Vijaya Daśamī* is observed there and the collector makes offerings to Lord Mahākāl. He, on behalf of Lord Mahākāl and with his blessings, cuts the Śamī tree. Then the effigies of Rāvaṇa and Kumbhakarṇa are burnt. The Mahākāl procession, after observing the *pūjan*, returns to the temple traversing the whole city.

Śāradā pūnam is also observed in the Mahākāl temple. It is considered to be the best full moon night of the year, when the moon showers *amṛta* (nectar). Milk is offered to Lord Mahākāl and then kept in moonlight. After three hours, the milk is brought and distributed among the devotees present. Some Āyurvedic medicines are also exposed to moonlight on this date for it is believed that this would increase the effectiveness of the medicines.

Rūpa Caudas is observed on the fourteenth day of the dark half of the month of *Kārtika*. The *liṅga* is specially cleaned and *annakūṭa* is performed during *bhasmāratī pūjan*. Only after its performance at Mahākāl is *annakūṭa* observed in other temples. After this the *liṅga* is covered with a thick layer of *bhāṅg* which remains up to ten o' clock in the morning. The entry of the devotees to the *sanctum-sanctorum* is prohibited for the period. Warm water is used for bathing Lord Mahākāl, which is done only on this day in the year. Pouring water is stopped till observance of *annakuṭa* at twelve noon. Sweets of *māvā* and *ṛtufala* (seasonal fruits) are included in the *annakuṭa* ceremony.

Dīwālī is observed by illuminating the temple complex. The main temple is decorated with chains of electric bulbs as replicas of *dīā* (earthen lamps). In the year 1979, two rows of *dīās* were kindled from the main gate to the *garbhagṛha* through the courtyard, *dālān* and stairs. Few hundred *dīās* were illuminated and the programme was flashed in the newspapers. This attracted people in large numbers. More people means more offerings, more *pūjan* and more *dāna*, and so it increases the earnings of the *pujarīs* and *paṇḍas*. Such arrangements, however, incur heavy expenditure though there remains the expectation of good earnings. This was planned by the *pujārīs*. The temple then was partially under government supervision.

On *Vaikuṇṭha Caudas* day (fourteenth day of the bright half of *Kārtika*) is observed *Hari-Hara-bheṇṭ* (meeting of Lord Hari or Viṣṇu and Lord Hara or Śiva). The Mahākāl procession goes to Gopāl Mandir, where Lord Mahakal is worshipped by the *pujārīs* of Gopāl Mandir with *tulasī* leaves. *Tulasī* leaves are used in Viṣṇu-worship only. Lord Viṣṇu is worshipped by Mahākāl *pujārīs* with *bilva patra* which is otherwise used for *Śivapūjan*. Lord Gopāl accompanies Lord Mahākāl to see him off. This is done at midnight (zero hour). *Kārtik melā* is the biggest fair of the year in Ujjain and it observed on the full moon day. People from distant villages come, offer *dīā* to the river Śiprā, take a bath at holy Śiprā and have a *darśana* of Lord Mahākāl. The ladies float *dīā* in Śiprā waters. There is also an animal fair, typical of its kind where along with the trade of other domesticated animals, donkeys are sold and purchased.

On all the Mondays in the month of *Kārtika*, the *Mahākāl savārī* is taken out. The palanquin of Lord Mahākāl is taken out in a procession to Rāmghāṭ and back to the temple. People make offerings en route.

Bhairavas are the creation of Lord Śiva; they are part of him. *Bhairava aṣṭamī* falls on the eighth day of the bright half of the next month. The *savārī* of Lord Kālabhairava, the chief among the Bhairavas, is taken out. Bhairavas at Mahākāl temple are specially worshipped on this occasion. Mahākāl as the greatest Bhairava is worshipped specially. *Til-sankrānti* is observed on the last day of the month of *Pauṣa. Tillī laḍḍu* is the special item prepared and offered to Lord Mahākāl.

Mahā Śivarātri is the largest festival celebrated in the Mahākāl temple. Preparations are made a month earlier. It falls on the fourteenth day of the dark half in the month of *Phālgun.* Cleaning and sweeping the whole temple premises, repair works, and decorations are done a month in advance. The whole temple is illuminated with electric lights and the old *jhaṇḍā* is replaced by a new one. It is observed as *navarātra* (nine-day celebration): it continues for nine days from the fifth day of the dark half of the month of *Phālgun* to the fourteenth day (*Śivarātri*). Decorative gates are erected and detailed arrangements are made to manage the rush of the devotees. The collector of Ujjain remains in charge of the arrangements and supervises them personally. During the period, *kathā pravacana* (religious discourses) by learned persons and *paṇḍits* are arranged. Some of them do it free of charge as a service to Lord Mahākāl. *Laghurudrābhiṣeka* and *Vaidika pūjan* by ten brāhmaṇas and an *ācārya* (Laxmīnārāyaṇa Vyās) are performed daily. In the evenings a new type of *śṛṅgāra* is done for Lord Mahākāl. Any performance (*pūjan, abhiṣeka,* etc.) during this period has additional importance and so there is a rush of devotees daily. Decorations, *śṛṅgāra,* religious discourses attract people from distant areas. The various *śṛṅgāras* made during this period include *tāṇḍava śṛṅgāra, Jerī śṛṅgāra* (headgear of *Jerī*).. *Umā-Maheśvar jhāṅkī, Man-Maheśvar jhāṅkī, ghaṭāṭop śṛṅgāra, Śeṣanāth śṛṅgāra* and *vastra śṛṅgāra.*

On *Śivarātri* day, the temple opens at 1:30 in the morning and *bhasmāratī pūjan* is performed. A special *āratī,* longer than usual, is done and this is the best *āratī* of the year. Garlands of *bor* fruit and *dhaturā* flower or fruit are offered and this is a must for this day. *Nitya pūjans* are performed as usual with the exception of *śayana ārati.* The temple remains open for the devotees throughout the night. Special police arrangements are made and two magistrates remain posted there. Additional counters are opened for the sale of coupons for the ritual performances. The *pujārīs* and *paṇḍās* invite their relatives to assist them on this occasion, and they are paid in cash and kind for their services.

It is a great affair for the devotees, the temple, the administration and Ujjain. Endless streams of visitors have a *darśana* of Lord Mahākāl. The old corridor and doors, being narrow, are kept closed for the visitors. The devotees are diverted through the newly constructed spacious and airy passage and underground *sabhāmaṇḍapa.* One has to wait for a long time in the line to have *darśana.* Between twelve at midnight and six in the morning, four *pūjans* with *rudrābhiṣeka* in each of the four *praharas* are performed. This is the special *pūjan* for the *Śivarātri* festival. After this, the *seharā kā śṛṅgāra* (decoration with flower garlands) of Lord Mahākāl is performed. In this garlands (of about fifty kilograms) are used which touch the ceiling. They are arranged in a characteristic way. This is done after *abhiṣeka pūjan* at five in the morning and kept for *darśana* till eleven in the morning. It attracts a great number of devotees and all the usual *pūjans*, including *bhasmāratī*, remain suspended during this time. At twelve midday, the *bhasmāratī pūjan* is performed. *Prātaḥkālīna pūjan* is performed after *bhasmāratī* and it is a special arrangement made on this occasion only. The eleven brāhmaṇas who do *laghūrudrābhiṣeka* for the last nine days are given a free meal and presented with fruits and *dakṣiṇā.*

The following day (second day of the bright half) all the five masks (used on occasions throughout the year) are arranged in the *jaladhārī* and this is known as *pañca-mukuṭa-kā-darśana.* It is done in the evening. It attracts the devotees and marks the end of the *Śivarātri* festival.

Holī, the spring festival popular in the whole of the land north of the Vindhyas, is observed on the full moon day of *Phālgun*. This festival is popular as *dhulaṇḍī* in Mālwā. A day earlier, the *Holikā* is burnt in the evening in various parts of the city. The *Holikā* is also burnt in the Mahākāl temple area as symbolic of the burning of the evil powers. A story tells us that *Holikā*, the evil spirit, was burnt by *agni* (fire) while Prahlāda, the Viṣṇu devotee, remained unaffected. On the *dhulaṇḍī* day, *gulāla* and colour are smeared on Lord Mahākāl. As Mahākāl is their protector, lord and deity the people observe the festival with their lord. *Savārī* (procession) is taken to the Śiprā *ghāṭs* and *Ger* (procession) is taken out from Bhāgsipurā and Sinhapuri (brāhmaṇa-dominated areas with very few people from other castes — which are not considered low). This procession reaches the Mahākāl temple where they are received by the *pujārīs*. An adequate amount of *bhāṅg* mixture is kept for their consumption. They dance and display martial arts such as stick playing. After this, the *Ger* participants return to their houses.

Besides these, some types of rituals are performed by the devotees and pilgrims eager to have a successful pilgrimage (*nai mithik*). They do it prior to a pilgrimage. There is a fixed rate of payment for such performances. Twenty-three recognised and listed *paṇḍās* are there to perform it and it is their exclusive right. The devotees are given receipts for the amount specified for the ritual concerned, on the production of which the *paṇḍā* performs the *pūjan*. Seventy-five per cent of the amount is given to the *paṇḍā* committee for distribution among the *paṇḍās* and one-fourth is retained for the maintenance of the other staff. The following are the types of performances:

1. *Sāmānya pūjan*
Pūrṇokta pūjan
2. *Ek mahimnā stotra*
3. *Ekādaśa mahimnā stotra*

Vaidika or vedokta pūjan

4. *Ekadarśinī namak camak*
5. *Laghurudrābhiṣeka*
6. *Mahārudrābhiṣeka*
7. *Atirudrābhiṣeka*

Sāmānya pūjan is a ritual which incurs one rupee and twenty-five paisa (Re 1. 25). A brāhmaṇa recites *mahimnā stotra* once in *ek mahimnā stotra.* This costs rupees two and a half (Rs. 2.50). In *ekādaśa mahimnā, ṣoḍaśopacāra pūjan* and *abhiṣeka* of Lord Mahākāl is done through recitation of *mahimnā stotra* by eleven brāhmaṇas simultaneously. The rate one has to pay for it is twenty-one rupees (Rs. 21). A brāhmaṇa does *abhiṣeka* of Lord Mahākāl with Rudrapāṭha in *ekadarśinī namak camak* which incurs rupees seven (Rs. 7). *Laghurudrābhiṣeka* is a big affair. It is done by ten brāhmaṇas and an *ācārya,* and it takes about three hours to be completed. It involves *abhiṣeka* with *rudrapāṭha* and *ṣoḍaśopacāra pūjan* for which one has to pay rupees one hundred and twenty-one (Rs. 121). For performing *mahārudrābhiṣeka, laghurudrābhiṣeka* is done for eleven days. One has to spend rupees thirteen hundred and thirty-one (Rs. 1331) for this. If *laghurudrābhiṣeka* is performed for one hundred and twenty-one days at a stretch, then it is called *atirudrābhiṣeka.* This is done at the rate of rupees one hundred and twenty-one (Rs. 121) per day. It is very rarely performed. There are two other kinds of rituals sometimes performed known as *bhāt-pūjan* and *ghṛt-pūjan.* The former is popular, while the latter one has been performed only once during the last thirty years. In *bhāt-pūjan* the *laghurudrābhiṣeka* is performed, then the *liṅga* and *jaladhārī* is covered with a thick coat of rice mixed with milk and *ghī.* A facial form is given with the help of rice paste to the south face of the holy *liṅga.* This *bhāt* (rice) thus offered is later taken by the *mahant* of the *Mahānirvāṇī akhāḍā* and distributed among the devotees and beggars as *prasād*. In *ghṛt-pūjan*, the frozen *ghī* slices are used in the same way to ornament Lord Mahākāl in addition to performing the normal *laghurudrābhiṣeka*. This attracts the devotees in a big way and the news is released to the press for wide publicity. A number of visitors crowd the temple. In all the rituals and decorations the south face of the holy *liṅga* is used as Lord Mahākāl is stated to be *Dakṣiṇa mūrti*. The *tāntrikas* are associated with the worship of this form of Lord Śiva.

IV

There are three kinds of brāhmaṇas who offer services to the pilgrims in the temple, i.e., *paṇḍā*, *pujārī*, and others who perform readings and recitations of sacred texts on request or otherwise. The *paṇḍās* and *pujārīs* have the hereditary right over these services.

Mahākāl *pujārīs* belong to Śrigauḍa Brāhmaṇa groups, have a common descent and are *patrikins*. Previously there was a Teleṅga brāhmaṇa who was the chief priest. It is said that he was originally from a village in Andhra Pradesh (Telengānā area) near the Mahārāṣtra border located on the bank of river Godāvarī and the *pujārīs* were his assistants. Following the entry of an untouchable into the temple, the chief priest left the temple and the other *pujārīs* became solely in charge of *pūjan*. Now they get rupees two thousand (Rs. 2000) as remuneration from the Mahākāl Samiti which is divided into sixteen shares. During the last *kumbha melā* (1980), a special sanction of twenty-five per cent of the total collection was made for the *pujārīs*. The right is inherited equally by all the brothers, but sisters and daughters have no claim. For ritual worship, the male primogeniture is observed. There are three seats in the Mahākāl *garbhagṛha* for the *pujārīs*, two on the west of *jaladhārī* and the other on the eastern part of *jaladhārī*. The western seats are exchanged after a year. Again, the southern-western seat and southern-eastern seat is exchanged after every month. [The year is counted from *Kārtik pūnam* and the month is observed according to the local calendar (*Vikram Samvat*)]. On the southern-eastern seat, the one-fourth (*cār-ānī*) shareholder group is concentrated. Western seats are exchanged among the members of the three-fourth (*bārā-ānī*) shareholder group. The *pujārīs* are meant to wear yellow robes and cannot use any stitched garments. This is the identity of the Mahākāl *pujārīs* and in Ujjain they constitute the chief *pujārī* group of the Śiva temples. They are also the *pujārīs* of the *caurāsī liṅgas* of Ujjain. Most of them live in Siṁhapurī and in the areas close to the Mahākāl temple. A group lives in Śani *gali* near Kailāśa theatre and another group lives near 'sarāfā' (jewellery market). The latter group is of mainly the *pujārīs* of several Viṣṇu temples. The Śrīgauḍ brāhmaṇas have an organisation here. The Mahākāl *pujārī* enjoys a high status in Ujjain and he proudly states his professional capacity on his name-plate. They claim to be migrants from some place in Kaśhmīr, who arrived with a ruler to settle in this place. They are one of the *pañca gauḍa* group of brāhmaṇas. Śrī means goddess Lakṣmī and she is their tutelary goddess. One among them has been appointed as the official priest by the Mahākāl committee and he is remunerated for his services. There are two assistant *pujārīs* selected from the *paṇḍās*, who also get remuneration from the Mahākāl Samiti. The *pujārīs* have a *samiti* to look after their interests.

The other important brāhmaṇa group in the Mahākāl temple is that of the Mahākāl *paṇḍās*. There are as many as twenty-three *paṇḍās* who have inherited the right. They belong to two brāhmaṇa groups — Śrīgauḍ and Gūjargauḍ. These two groups do not always see eye to eye, but common interests have them united. A *samiti* of the *paṇḍās* puts forward their demands to the authorities. An attempt has also been made to bring the *pujārīs* and *paṇḍās* under a common banner. These *paṇḍās* perform the *pūjan, mahimnā* or *abhiṣeka* for the devotees on payment by the devotee. A receipt is issued from the counter on which the name of the *paṇḍā* who has to serve is written. This receipt is shown to the specified *paṇḍā* who performs the *pūjan*. He keeps the *pūjan sāhitya* (items necessary for *pūjan*) always ready with him. Besides, they have *jajmāns* living in distant towns and cities and a record is maintained. They perform the required *pūjan* for their *jajmān* on payment, and make arrangements for food and shelter as well as perform rituals for a visiting *jajmān*. For any *abhiṣeka* in Mahākāl, however, they are to accept a receipt from the counter on payment. Of the total accumulation from the receipts, the *paṇḍās* get three-fourths of the total amount. One-fourth is retained with the Mahākāl Samiti for maintenance costs. Payment is made every week, and the money is given to the secretary of the *paṇḍā samiti*. Some people in the habit of visiting the temple daily develop a stable relationship with the *paṇḍās*. Besides the *pūjan*, the *paṇḍās* sit in the *dālān* (*kūṇḍa* side *sabhāgṛha*). There are seventeen *takhtas*. Hereditary rules are observed for the right of sitting on those *takhtas* and in case of several brothers they sit in turn — for five hours or more or less. They keep flowers, *bilva patra*, sandal paste and other required items of worship. By providing these things and applying *ṭikā* on the forehead of the devotees, and also supplying *loṭās* (metal pots) used for pouring water on the divine *liṅga*, they earn some money. They also look after the belongings of the devotee when he/she is inside the temple and in return for these services, the devotees pay some amount to them. These *paṇḍas* also develop contacts with the pilgrims. Sometimes some devotees take a vow or wish to give *dāna* to brāhmaṇas. The *paṇḍās* then stand in a queue to accept the *dāna*. To protect the right of the *paṇḍā* organisation, the *paṇḍās* show their presence at least for a few hours of the day (mainly morning and evening) during lean months. Some of the well-known *paṇḍās* of Ujjain who are not attached to Mahākāl Temple and who are mostly in the Śiprā *ghāṭs* have been known to perform *pūjan, abhiṣeka* for their *jajmāns*. However, they have no right to sit over the *takhtas*.

Śrīgauḍ *paṇḍās* and *pujārīs* are closely related. Gujargauḍ brāhmaṇas attached to the Mahakal temple are also closely related.

There is a third group of brāhmaṇas, which includes various brāhmaṇa groups, such as Śrīgauḍ, Gujargauḍ, Audicyagauḍ Caturvedī, etc. By profession they are *kathāvācak*, or perform *pāṭh* (reading, reciting) of sacred texts, do *jāpa* (uttering name of particular god or goddess several times), etc. — services which are not rendered by the *paṇḍās* or *pujārīs* against payment. But these people need to have good relations with the *paṇḍās* and *pujārīs* and so they always support them. The temple is the place where they get the devotees or *jajmāns*. Even when they do not have any instructions for *pāṭha*, etc. they do so on their own to attract the people and make them aware that brāhmaṇas for such purposes are available in the Mahākāl temple. Some are efficient in their profession and earn a reasonable amount. Those who are interested in feeding brāhmaṇas also come here, make contacts with the brāhmaṇas here and pay them according to their economic ability in addition to *dakṣiṇā*. There are some more or less fixed rates for specific performances.

Saints also take shelter here for a day or two in the course of their travels all over the country. The devotees give cooked and uncooked food to these people and thereby earn their blessings as well as some *puṇya*.

V

The visitors to this great temple may be categorised as daily visitors, incidental or occasional visitors and pilgrims. The daily visitors are mainly the urbanites of Ujjain and some daily commuters. It is part of their daily routine to visit the temple. Mostly they pour water, and offer flowers and other things. Only on special occasions do they go for *abhiṣeka pūjan*. The second category includes visitors who have come to Ujjain for some other purpose and incidentally pay a visit. People from the towns and cities as well as from the rural areas of Mālwā come on special occasions like *Śivarātri*, *Nāgpañcamī*, or fairs such as *Somtī amāvasyā*, or *Śani amāvasyā*, *Kārtik melā*, *Śrāvaṇa savārī*, *Pañcakośī*, etc. The largest congregation is on the eve of the *kūmbha melā* held everv twelve years. The strength of the devotees assembled for *darśana* of Lord Mahākāl increases with the importance of the festival. Festivals which are of pan-Indian importance attract people from distant areas. For festivals of local popularity it is mostly the Mālvīs who assemble. The third category is that of the pilgrims. This is not to suggest that the visitors of other categories are not pilgrims. The distinction has been suggested on the basis of the motives of the visitors. This category includes those visitors who come to this temple depending on their programme for visiting various pilgrim centres, and singly, with family members or in groups (by hired buses or as arranged by the travel agencies). There are various types of pilgrimage or *yātrā* like *Cāra-dhāma yātrā*, *Dvādaśa jyotirliṅga yātrā*, etc. After the harvest, the people from the rural areas go on a pilgrimage. They hire a bus and visit the important centres of pilgrimage. Such groups come from various parts of Rājasthān, Gujarāt, Mahārāṣṭra and other states. They put cereals (*jwār*, wheat or *bājrā*) near the *dānapeṭī* instead of money as *dāna*.

The distant visitors live in hotels or *dharmaśālās*. There are more than fifty *dharmaśālās* in Ujjain. Influential castes have their own *dharmaśālās* with a temple to serve their customers. They provide food at subsidised rates and accommodation free or at nominal charges. The daily visitors who are mainly from this city maintain an air of religiosity in the temple and in the city too. A man without a *ṭikā* mark is not liked and the *ṭikā* mark indicates that he has performed the *pūjā* or visited some temple. Many are found having a *rudrākṣamālā*, and long hair and there are several bearded men. Various organisations, shops, etc. have been set up in the name of Lord Mahākāl and in buses and other public vehicles there are photographs of Lord Mahākāl. The citizens very proudly speak to the outsider about the sacredness of the *kṣetra*, about Lord Mahākāl and the *kumbha melā*. These factors are expected to influence the outsider. *Paṇḍās* move around the city and people are found to take a bath or meditate throughout the day on Śiprā *ghāṭs*. The citizens play a great role in perpetuating the status of Ujjain as a sacred city.

VI

Since the year 1978 (30th October), the local administration has taken up the management of the temple following a court verdict. In accordance to this a Mahākāl Samiti has been constituted for overall supervision, which has seven members with the collector of Ujjain as the Chairman. Taking into consideration the importance of the city as a pilgrim centre and the existence of various temples, a separate department has been formed and the responsibility has been given to a *Nāyab Tehsīldār*. The sub-divisional officer is also primarily responsible for supervision of various works and he functions as the secretary of the Mahākāl Samiti. The Administrator of the Municipal Corporation and the Executive Engineer of the State Government Public Works Department are also members. The rest of the members are from the elite. This committee takes the vital decisions and the *pujārīs* and *paṇḍās* are also consulted. The following are the regular employees of the *samiti* who look after the daily affairs of the temple:

Manager : He has a status equivalent to that of *Tehsīldār* in the revenue department. The present manager is the retired commissioner of the Municipal Corporation. He supervises the work and does not take any remuneration.

Assistant Manager : He is the accountant and is available from morning to evening. He is there to solve problems or to inform the sub-

		divisional officer and act according to his instructions. He is a retired person who gets remuneration for the work done.
Koṭhārī	:	He is the storekeeper. It is a part-time job for which he gets an allowance. Primarily he is an employee of the Divisional Commissioner's office and has been deputed to do this job.
Counter Clerk	:	There are three persons with rotational duty hours and they get paid for their services.
Nirīkṣaka	:	Five *nirīkṣaka* remain in the Mahākāl *garbhagṛha* and keep a watch that the *caḍhotrī* (cash offering) and other things offered are collected and deposited at the *samiti* office. Their duty hours also change (morning or evening) every week. They keep close watch so that the *yātrīs* are not deceived. Two homeguard personnel help them in their work and they get payment for their services.
Pujārī	:	He is one of the Mahākāl *pujārīs* who serves as the official *pujārī* and receives monthly remuneration.
Sahāyaka pujārī	:	There are two *pujārīs* to assist the chief *pujārī*, who also get a salary.
Khalāsī	:	There are five of them. They keep the whole area clean and are responsible for the disposal of offered flowers and *bilva patra*. Also, they throw away the stored water offered to Lord Mahākāl from the accumulation chamber from time to time. They are employed on a monthly-pay basis.

Cook : A lady cook is employed to cook the *bhog* and she gets remuneration every month.

Besides, there are suppliers of *bilva patra*, flowers and other items of offering. A *maśālcī* and a *nagārcī* or drum-beater (both traditional servants) and an electrician also serve. Two *safāivālās* are there for keeping the whole complex clean. There are other traditional servants like *copdār* (who announces the arrival of Lord Mahākāl), *kahārs* (who carry the palanquin of Lord Mahākāl during *savārīs*). They get some money in the form of land grants and have the exclusive right over the coins which are thrown by the devotees on the palanquin of Mahākāl during the procession (coins which miss the palanquin and fall on the road).

The following are the sources of income for meeting the maintenance expenditures:

1. From *caḍhotrī* (offerings in cash and kind), twenty-five per cent of the cash is paid to the *pujārīs* in addition to their fixed amount of Rupees two thousand (Rs. 2000).

2. Devotees from distant places send money through money orders as *dāna*.

3. Rent from the shops.

4. Financial grants from Holkar (Indore) and Powar (Dewās).

5. Substantial amounts of money collected from each *savārī* in the month of *Śrāvaṇa* and *Kārtika*.

6. The highest amount in cash and also kind, however, comes from the collection during *Siṁhastha* (*kumbha melā*). (During the last *Kumbha melā* in 1980 the cash collection according to rough approximation was nearly rupees one-and-a-half lakh). After giving twenty-five per cent of it to the *pujārīs*, there was more than rupees one lakh in credit. A fixed deposit of rupees one lakh has been opened in the name of Lord Mahākāl.

The temple has assets in land, cash amount, valuable stones, ornaments of gold, silver and other items like cloth, etc.

List of sacred *caurāsī liṅga* and their location in different parts of Ujjain *kṣetra*:

Sl. No.	*Name*	*Location*
1.	Agasteśvar	Behind Harsiddhi temple
2.	Guheśvar	Near Piśāca Mukteśvar temple
3.	Dhuṇḍeśvar	Under Rāmsirī (Rāmghāṭ)
4.	Ḍamarukeśvar	Above Rāmsirī (Rāmghāṭ)
5.	Anādi Kalpeśvar	Mahākāl complex
6.	Swarnajaleśvar	Mahākāl complex
7.	Tribisṭapeśvar	Mahākāl complex
8.	Kapāleśvar	Biloṭipura
9.	Swargadvāreśvar	Nāliā bākhāl
10.	Karkoṭeśvar	Harsiddhi temple
11.	Siddheśvar	Sidhvaṭ complex
12.	Lokpāleśvar	Harsiddhi Darvājā
13.	Mankāmaneśvar	Gandharvatī
14.	Kuṭumbeśvar	Singpuri Darvājā
15.	Indra Dumneśvar	Modī-kī-galī
16.	Īśāṇeśvar	Modī-kī-galī
17.	Apsareśvar	Modī-kī-galī
18.	Kalkāleśvar	Modī-kī-galī

Sl. No.	*Name*	*Location*
19.	Nāgcandreśvar	Paṭnī Bājār
20.	Pratihāreśvar	Near Nāg Candreśvar temple
21.	Kukkuṭeśvar	Gandharvatī
22.	Karkaṭeśvar	Khaṭikbāḍā
23.	Maghnadeśvar	Sarāfā Bājār
24.	Mahālayeśvar	Khatrībāḍā
25.	Mukteśvar	Khatrībāḍā
26.	Someśvar	Biloṭipura
27.	Anarkeśvar	Makoḍiā ām
28.	Jaṭeśvar	Gayā koṭhā
29.	Rāmeśvar	Satīdarvājā
30.	Cāmaneśvar	Puruṣottamsāgar
31.	Khaṇḍeśvar	Khilchipura
32.	Paṭṭaneśvar	Khilchipura
33.	Ānandeśvar	Near Cakratīrtha
34.	Kanṭhaḍeśvar	Sidhvaṭ complex
35.	Indreśvar	Biloṭipura
36.	Markaṇḍeśvar	Viṣṇusāgar (Aṅkpaṭ complex)
37.	Viveśvar	Near Ranj (Aṅkpaṭ complex)
38.	Kusumeśvar	Near Ranj (Aṅkpaṭ complex)
39.	Akrureśvar	Near Aṅkpaṭ Darvājā

Sl. No.	Name	Location
40.	Kuṇḍeśvar	Gomtī Kuṇḍa (Aṅkpaṭ complex)
41.	Lampeśvar	Haḍas Sāgar (Behind Kāla Bhairava)
42.	Gaṅgeśvar	Khaḍgota Saṅgam
43.	Aṅgrakeśvar	Near Maṅgalnāth temple complex
44.	Uttareśvar	Near Maṅgalnāth temple complex
45.	Trilocaneśvar	Namdarpura
46.	Vireśvar	Near Satyanārāyaṇa Mandir
47.	Nupureśvar	Deorīpeṭha
48.	Avayeśvar	Daorī Darvājā
49.	Prithukeśvar	In Kedāreśvar temple
50.	Sthāvareśvar	Near Kailāśa theatre
51.	Śūleśvar	Khaṭīkabāḍā
52.	Oṁkāreśvar	Khaṭīkabāḍā
53.	Viśveśvar	Khaṭīkabāḍā
54.	Nīlkaṇṭheśvar	Near Jāṭ-kā-kuān
55.	Sinheśvar	Near Gaṇapati in the Garh (fort)
56.	Rebanteśvar	Kārtik Chowk
57.	Ghaṇṭeśvar	Kārtik Chowk
58.	Prayāgeśvar	Cakratīrtha (crematorium)
59.	Singeśvar	Near *pīpal* tree in Khatrī bāḍā
60.	Mātaṅgeśvar	Piñjharwāḍī

Sl. No.	*Name*	*Location*
61.	Saubhāgyeśvar	Near Vidhvā Āśram
62.	Rūpeśvar	Siṁhapuri
63.	Dhanusāheśvar	Nayapurā
64.	Paśupateśvar	Jansapurā
65.	Brahameśvar	Khaṭikabaḍā
66.	Jalpeśvar	Somtīrtha
67.	Kedāreśvar	Near Sunārghāṭ
68.	Piśācamukteśvar	Rāmghāt
69.	Saṅgameśvar	Jairāmdās Śamirāmdās Dharmaśālā
70.	Durdhaneśvar	Gandharvatīrtha
71.	Prayāgeśvar	Harasiddhi Darvājā
72.	Candrādityeśvar	Mahākāl complex
73.	Karveśvar	Near Kālabhairava temple
74.	Rajāsthaleśvar	Bhāgsipura
75.	Wadāleśvar	Sidhvaṭ complex
76.	Āmneśvar	Rāmghāṭ
77.	Puṣpadatteśvar	Pandhoriba
78.	Avimukteśvar	Near Rupeśvar temple
79.	Hanumukteśvar	Near Gadkālikā temple
80.	Svapaneśvar	Mahākāl complex
81.	Svapaneśvar	Mahākāl complex

Sl. No.	Name	Location
82.	Kāyābaroneśvar	Karankakla Kheḍī
83.	Bilkeśvar	Umodia village
84.	Durdureśvar	Jethal village

There are a few Śiva temples intricately linked with Lord Mahākāl like the Maṅgalnāth temple, Sidhvaṭ, etc. The Mahākāl *pujārīs* go to Maṅgalnāth for the performance of some specific rituals and the *mahant* of Maṅgalnāth gives some portion of the *caḍhotrī* collected to the Mahākāl *pujārīs*. There is no fixed ratio and it is given as a lumpsum. Sidhvaṭ is considered as the chief officer of Lord Mahākāl in Ujjain. Besides, there are the sacred eighty-four *liṅgas* mentioned in the *Skanda Purāṇa*. Each *liṅga* has a myth and it is aptly commented that there is hardly anything in India which has not a myth. These eighty-four *liṅgas* are believed to be the incarnations of Lord Śiva which became prominent following specific incidents. *Darśana* of these *liṅgas* and making offerings to them constitute a recognised form of pilgrimage in Ujjain and it is popular as *caurāsī-liṅga-kī-yātrā*. Mahākāl *pujārīs* are also the *pujārīs* of these temples. Some of these are very popular like the four temples in four directions that are considered as Dvārapāla of Mahākāl *kṣetra*. In the Mahākāl complex there are four of these temples. Anādikalpeśvar temple is well constructed and draws the attention of pilgrims. But some distant temples are uncared for. They are not cleaned except on some occasions. Kāleśvar Mahādeva temple is looked after by the saints of the *tāntrika* order. There are some figurines in the temple showing erotic forms. Maintenance of this temple is very poor and some stray dogs have made it their home. The *yātrīs* of *caurāsī liṅga* get them cleaned during their visits and make the offerings.

5

The Link

Melas, Festivals, Folk Theatre

I

UJJAIN is one of the four venues on earth for the *kumbha melā*. The origin of this fair was perhaps the inspiration for holding religious congresses at regular intervals. It is believed that there are twelve sites for the *kumbha melā*, eight in heaven and four on earth. At present the great fair takes place at Haridvār, Prayāga, Ujjain and Nāsik. It cannot be ascertained when the tradition began. It cannot be said when the practice of holding this *melā* at the instance of Jupiter entering Leo started at Ujjain. However, it is certain that these fairs originally started not earlier than the time when the system of the twelve astronomical signs of the Zodiac was introduced to India. This happened most probably in the third century BC.

But the idea of such a religious congress is still older. It originated in the Vedic period. The learned persons used to assemble at some place from time to time to discuss theological, philosophical and religious subjects for months together. Such assemblies were then called *Brahmasatra* (a session of lectures on supreme spirit) or *Sarasvatīsatra* (a session of learned lectures). Their mention is found in *Bṛhadāraṇyaka* and *Āśvalāyana Śrauta Sūtra* and in other Vedic compilations. In the Buddhist period, *mahāsabhās* of learned followers of Buddhism were held in the same line and on the basis of the *Brahmasatra* or *Sarasvatīsatra.* With the change of time and socio-political conditions, these *satras* have been developed into periodic fairs or these fairs might have been started on the basis of the traditional *satras*. This tradition of holding a periodic fair facilitates easy exchange of ideas among people from different parts of the country and paves the way for maintaining mutual good will and harmony. Such fairs were held at centres of pilgrimage which were no doubt the seats of learning and the rendezvous of spiritual and intellectual giants. How Ujjain became the seat of this fair cannot be traced. It is, however, certain that Ujjain was a centre of learning in ancient India. The temple of Lord Mahākāl and the sacred river Śiprā which flows north must have played a great role in the selection of Ujjain as the venue. It was a centre of *ṛṣis* in ancient India. According to *paurāṇika* descriptions, the city of Avantikā came up following the congregation of hermits and sages in Mahākālavana. The Viśvakarmā (the divine architect) constructed the original temple of Mahākāl at the gate of which a huge bell used to hang from gold chains.

About the *Kumbha melā* the popular myth says that there was *samudra-manthana* (churning of sacred sea) in which both the *suras* (gods) and *asuras* (demons) participated. Vāsukī, the divine Snake King served as the rope of the churning rod, a hill placed on a sacred tortoise. In the process, several things evolved. Finally goddess Lakṣmī came with the *amṛta kumbha* (pot of nectar). Both the *suras* and *asuras* were after it to gain immortality by consuming some nectar. There was a fierce fight between these two groups. Jayanta, the son of Indra, carried it away, guarded by Sūrya and other gods. They let the *kumbha* touch the earth at four places where a few drops of nectar fell. Ujjain is one of the four places. Because of this incident these places became very sacred and hence the venue of a great congress for discussion on philosophies.

In Ujjain, one of the most holy centres for the Hindus, the *kumbha melā* is held after every twelve years. Unlike Haridvār and Prayāg, there is only *Pūrṇakūmbha* and no five-yearly *ardhakūmbha* congregation in Ujjain. *Kumbha melā* in Ujjain is known locally as *siṁhastha melā*. The observance of the *kumbha melā* at a particular time depends on ten considerations and one of the considerations for this *melā* is entering of the planet Bṛhaspati in *siṁharāśi* (hence the name, *siṁhastha*). The ten factors for the *kumbha mela* in Ujjain are (1) *Baisākh* month, (2) bright half, (3) full moon day, (4) Sūrya in *meṣa rāśi*, (5) Candra in *tulā rāśi*, (6) Bṛhaspati in *siṁhā rāśi*, (7) *swāti nakṣatra*, 8) *vyatipāt yoga*, (9) *somvār*, (10) Ujjain on the bank of *uttarvāhinī* Śiprā. These conditions mostly coincide given a twelve-year periodic interval. There are differences of opinion about the date of *siṁhastha melā* mainly between the *Vaiṣṇava* saints and those who belong to *Śaiva sampradāya*. The former insist on the periodic interval while the latter stress the position of the solar constellation. Owing to the disagreements the *Siṁhastha* was twice celebrated (in 1956–57 and in 1968–69) separately in consecutive years. In 1980 the various saint organisations arrived at a joint communique. They compromised and decided to celebrate in the same year, date and time. And so, there was an unprecedented rush in that year.

The saints and saint organisations are primarily concerned with *siṁhastha*, for which there are several reasons. Firstly, during such congregations the *maṇḍaleśvar*s and *mahāmaṇḍaleśvar*s or *mahant*s and other organisational heads assemble at the place. So election to various offices of the *akhāḍā*s takes place at this congregation. In this *melā* the *akhāḍā*s remain in the forefront and initiation to various stages and recruitment to *akhāḍā*s takes place (like *Vijayahoma*, etc.). The colourful processions are taken out to show the resources of the organisation and also the might in number of followers and spiritual achievement. All the organisations thrive on supremacy and the main polarisation is under the banners, *Vaiṣṇava sampradāya* and *Śaiva sampradāya*. There have been incidents of fierce fighting between the saints of these two groups resulting in loss of lives (in Haridvār, during the rule of Emperor Jehāngīr). However, there is no such extreme case to relate with reference to Ujjain. There was the practice of a saint shouting *jai śiprāji*, diping his *niśhāna* (flag) in the water and taking a bath. This was to announce the beginning of the bath. But the announcer and some others died soon after under mysterious conditions and this was believed to be the work of the *caunsaṭh* (sixty-four) *yoginīs* of Ujjain. Such a practice of announcing has, however, been prohibited by the local administration since the *siṁhastha melā* of the fifties. The violence breaks out mainly on the issue of who will take the bath first. Armed police remain alert to meet the tense situation.

Siṁhastha melā is not an affair of Mālwā or the state administration alone; it is an affair of the whole country. The saint organisations have a countrywide network of units and there is a committee to take the decision about the date which is communicated to various units and *akhāḍās* who, in turn, inform their own branches spread in various pilgrim centres. And the saints attached to the *akhāḍās* or other organisations, or even independent saints start reaching this holy city about three months earlier. Their arrival gives the city a festive look and local units of the various *akhāḍās* and organisations make preparations much earlier. An *akhāḍā* makes arrangements for food and accommodation to the saints attached to that *akhāḍā*.

In 1980, altogether five dates were fixed for the auspicious dip — 31st March, 13th April, 15th April, 17th April and 19th April. The final *kūmbha snān* which is popular as *śāhī-snān* or the holy dip was fixed on 30th April. With the *snān* of 31st March, the *Siṁhastha* fair started and it culminated with the *śāhī-snān* on 30th April. For the whole month the saints of various organisations camped at Ujjain. From 1st May onwards, they started dispersing from Ujjain.

During the *siṁhastha* of 1980, about forty lakhs of people visited the holy city in a month's period. These included saints, pilgrims and traders from different parts of the country. Pilgrims were in a large number and the hotels, lodges and *dharamśālās* became so crowded that people had to sleep in open spaces. But the arrangements made in preparation of the mela were elaborate. A high power committee for the *melā* was formed with representatives from the state administration, saint organisations and local influential persons. Ujjain is a divisional headquarter and a divisional commissioner is posted there. A *melā* office was established more than a year ahead to look after the work on different fronts and coordinate them well. An officer of the Indian Administrative Service headed the organisation. Maximum stress was given on health, construction and widening of roads, construction of platforms and bridges over the railroad at two places, diverting the water of the Gambhīra river and occasional release of the water during the month-long *melā* period. Various temples were renovated, repaired on this occasion and several new constructions were taken up in the Mahākāl temple so as to meet the rush and accommodate the crowd of devotees. Śiprā *ghāṭ*s were extended and repaired at various places and the banks of Śiprā were dotted with temples and *ghāṭ*s. Renovation was done in this area and floating bridges were constructed to cross the river at various points. Arrangements were made for additional bus and train services. Temporary huts were constructed for the pilgrims. Vehicular traffic was banned inside the city limits and the central bus stand was shifted to the temporary bus stand outside the city. Temporary taps were installed at various places for drinking water and the supply was maintained round-the-clock. Other preparations like inoculation of the citizens at every entry to the city were made. A committee at the administrative level was formed with the divisional commissioner as the chairman. Heads of different departments were its members and every month a meeting of the committee used to be convened under the divisional commissioner in which the progress made in various works was assessed. An exhibition was organised by the local administration and plots were allotted to different religious organisations for their use as camp sights. Śaivites were accommodated on the west bank of the Śiprā and Vaiṣṇavites near the Aṅkpaṭ complex.

The traders also made preparations beforehand. They raised an adequate stock of cereals and other commodities of daily need. It was a time of booming business for those in the trade of idols, and other materials of worship like symbols (such as *yantras*), religious books, etc. Hotel and lodge owners raised the rate for accommodation about eight months earlier and provisions were made to accommodate (extra cots, etc.) more persons in a room. Rates of milk and milk products increased considerably though the local adminstration took positive steps like transporting milk from other areas to have control over the price hike.

It was a most important occasion for the priestly groups. During the period more *abhiṣekas*, *pūjan*, *yajñas* and other rituals were performed due to the presence of holy men and a large number of pilgrims. It was a period that brought a lot of earnings for the *Tīrtha-purohits*. But beforehand, to meet the needs of more *pujārīs and paṇḍās*, their relatives were invited to help them for a share of the earnings and an additional stock of *pūjan sāhitya* (items of worship) was arranged. Brāhmaṇas from the neighbouring areas and states camped for the period in Ujjain to cater to the needs of the pilgrims performing rituals. The *paṇḍās* later expressed satisfaction with the arrangements of the local administration and the flow of money from the visitors.

Akhāḍās, as said earlier, made preparations well in advance. The various saints and religious men were busy mainly in two ways. Firstly, they had their organisational responsibilities like electing an office bearer, installation of a person to a specific post and initiation, etc. Elected persons then arranged a *bhaṇḍārā* (feast) for the saints. Secondly, they remained busy in participating in religious discourses. Taking part in discussions, reciting and explaining the religious texts, performing *yajña* or other rituals and the like kept them busy throughout the month. Some of the *haṭha-yogīs* used to perform feats before the public to enthral them.

The people from rural Mālwā benefited in two ways — they had good earnings as well as an opportunity to listen to various godmen and have informal meetings with the pilgrims coming from other parts of the country. Strong networks maintained by the *akhāḍās* and other saint organisations contributed to the congregation of the *sādhus* from different pilgrim centres. These *sādhus* move from one pilgrim centre to the other attending *melās*. Taking a bath during *siṁhastha* is very auspicious and the *sādhus* do not miss this occasion.

II

Besides the *siṁhastha melā,* there are a few other *melās* and *yātrās* which involve people mainly from the sub-regions. These are the *Kārtik melā, Pañcakośī yātrā, Cāradvāra yātrā, Aṣṭatīrthī yātrā, Somtī* and *Śani amāvasyā*, etc. *Kārtik melā* is observed on the full moon day in the month of *Kārtik* (October-November). People from the rural areas, particularly the women-folk, come and float *dīās* (lamps) in Śiprā waters. It is a month-long programme. People take a bath in some holy places near their villages but the final dip on *Kārtik pūnam* in the Śiprā waters at Ujjain is important. On the eve there is a series of programmes arranged by the municipal authorities for entertainment, thus making it more popular. On the other bank of the Śiprā a space has been demarcated for the *melā.* Local authorities even try to popularise *Baisākhī pūnam.* Again there were proposals for an *Ardhakumbha* like that of Haridvār and

Prayāga after every five years. This, however, could not receive much support. *Kārtik melā* brings in a lot of earnings for the local traders. An attraction of this *melā* is the livestock fair organised on this occasion. Earlier it was a market for donkey trade, where asses were sold and purchased. Now it has taken the shape of a livestock market. So it attracts the farmers in great numbers from rural Mālwā.

This is also true of *yātrās*. There are four *Śaiva* temples in four directions which are called Dvārapālas of Ujjain *kṣetra*. People start the *yātrā* from Mahākāleśvar and visit the four Dvārapālas and make offerings. It involves mostly the people of Ujjain itself though the rural people from nearby areas also participate. This is popularly known as *cāradivāra yātrā*. In *Aṣṭatīrthi yātrā*, twenty-eight *tīrthas* are visited in Ujjain and offerings are made. People start their journey from Karkarāj Mahādeva temple in the southern part and end at Sidhvaṭ in the northern part. Participants are mostly rural people, though people from urban areas are also in sizeable strength. These two *yātrās* involve less time and strain. *Pañcakośī yātrā* is comparatively tough and has the participation of mainly the rural folk, with people from urban places constituting less than five per cent of the total number. People start from the Nāgcandreśvar Mahādeva temple in Paṭnibājār and go to the eastern Dvārapāla. From there they go to the southern Dvārapāla and the northern via the western Dvārapāla. They reach Rāmghāṭ via the eastern Dvārapāla. At every Dvārapāla they take a bath and make offerings. They halt at four places where arrangements are made by the local authorities for camping. During the *siṁhastha melā*, the number of participants shoots up. In 1980 it was more than a lakh participants which included the rural folk of Mālwā, the visiting pilgrims and also camping saints. The objective is to take a round of the *kṣetra*. It is outside the city limits. The villagers offer drinking water, *śarbat* (sweet drink) and tea to the pilgrims. These participants are considered as holy men. Caste distinctions do not come in the way. It is a tiresome journey and some fall sick. In such cases they are transported to the city and medical aid is provided. It is a regional affair and the participants are mainly from the rural areas of Mālwā. Only in the year of the *siṁhastha melā* do the outsiders participate. The tradition of taking a round of the *kṣetra* is not unique to Ujjain. It is also observed in other pilgrim centres (Sinha and Sarasvati, 1978). The rural people from different villages come in contact with each other. People from a particular village form a group and retain it till the end. They amuse themselves and others with devotional songs and singers from other villages sometimes join. Actually it provides an opportunity to the villagers to come out of their little world.

Amāvasyā is observed when it falls on the Monday (*somtī amāvasyā*) and on the Saturday (*śani amāvasyā*). In the former case, people take a bath in the muddy water (in summer or lean seasons) at Somtīrtha (it is a place on the opposite bank of Cakratīrtha which was the confluence of the Gandharvatī and Śiprā). They make offerings to the Someśvar Mahādeva temple. Ladies take only three rounds or one hundred and eight rounds of the neighbouring banian tree. They sing songs and offer water to the sacred tree. *Vaṭ* is believed to be the seat of Lord Śiva and so it is very sacred. After this they take the final bath at Rāmghāṭ, the sacredness of which draws them to this *ghāṭ*. Some groups of ladies take a round of the banian trees in this *ghāṭ* also. In *Śani amāvasyā* the rural people come in groups and take a bath at Triveṇī *ghāṭ* on the Śiprā bank near the Navagraha temple. After that they make offerings to Lord Śani at the Navagraha temple and offerings to other planet gods as well. But Śani is the prime Lord worshipped on that day. Even otherwise Saturday is the day observed for Lord Śani.

In both these *yātrās* or *melās* (fairs) the participants are predominantly rural folk coming from the villages of Mālwā. Tribals also participate in such fairs. The snake charmers and *naṭs* (dancer singers) attend these fairs and earn some money. The other beneficiaries of these *melās* are the *tīrtha purohits* and other priests. The devotees who visit the temples including Mahākāleśvar temple perform rituals through these brāhmaṇas who earn a handsome amount. Finally, *snān* is interlinked with *dāna* and *devadarśana*. One takes a bath and then donates something to brāhmaṇas and beggars and then has a *darśana* of his lord. *Dāna* to brāhmaṇas fetches more *puṇya* and there are specific items of *dāna* for specific occasions. For brāhmaṇas the material to be included in the *dāna* is also specified. In sacred texts, *dānagrahīta* has been given great importance particularly where the receiver is a brāhmaṇa. By accepting that *dāna* the brāhmaṇa paves the *dātā*'s way to heaven. So the pilgrims get benefited through the acceptance of such *dāna* by the Brāhmaṇas. *Dāna* is the most praised deed for a true Hindu. There is a sudden increase in the number of beggars at the site on these occasions. Like any other pilgrim centre of Ujjain's status, there are a number of beggars near the main temples in Ujjain. *Annadāna* is a specific *dāna* on *somti amāvasyā* fair. So both the sellers of cereals and the *dānagrahītas* are found at the *ghāṭs*. Normally neither of the groups is seen here. Sometimes the accumulated cereals of the beggars come to them via the seller and the pilgrim. These beggars also do not beg regularly and most of them come from nearby villages.

III

To understand the festivals and rituals of rural Mālwā, four villages were visited. The data has been mainly collected on the religious life of the people. Their awareness about Ujjain and their involvement with this holy city has been considered and data has been collected accordingly. The four villages are Sirolyā (Śājāpur district) in the east, Gajnīkheḍā on the west, Jalwā on the north and Kāṅkriyāpāl in the south. All are more or less of the same population size and multi-ethnic in composition and they are approximately equidistant from Ujjain. There are, in all, about thirty major castes. There are other communities as well. The castes include Brāhmaṇa, Gosāin, Gairi, Mālī, Nāī, Lohar, Bairāgī, Camār, Dhanuk, Balai, Naṭa, Bhīla (Tadbi), Telī, Sutar, Darjī, Paṭṭīdār,Kumhār, Rājpūt, Dholī. There are Jains and Muslims as well. Bairāgi, Rajput, Mali (traditionally included in the list of vegetarian castes) and the Sutar, Teli, Nāī are among those considered as primary castes in earlier times.

Gajnīkheḍā is to the west of Ujjain. It falls under the jurisdiction of Baḍanagar tehsil of Ujjain. Runija is the nearest large village from where there is a bus service to Ujjain. It plies once a day. Runija is also on the Indore-Ratlām meter-guage railroad. Our study village is about two miles from Runija and the railway station is a little further.

The various castes have their own *gotra bhairava* or *bherū* and *mātā*. The Bhīls, too, have their own *bherū* and *mātā* which they worship. They make offerings to their clan *bherū* on *Bhairū pūnam* in the month of *Āsāḍha* (June-July). *Mātā* is worshipped during the *Navarātra* festival in *Kuār* (September-October) month. There is a temple dedicated to Cāmuṇḍāmātā which is very important for not only Gajnīkheḍā but also for the villages in the neighbourhood. There is a fair during *Navarātra* festival which attracts a great crowd. The temple shows old construction and there are signs of serious damage. It is said that the temple was damaged during the Muslim attacks and since then reconstruction has not been done owing to the shortage of funds. But some construction has been done with donation from the villagers. There are various *bherū* who are worshipped for various purposes. *Grām bherū, kheḍā bherū* and the like are worshipped at the village level. Besides, there are temples dedicated to Viṣṇu, Nāg Mahārāja, Rāmdeojī, Devanārāyaṇajī, Śiva, Hanumānjī, Śītalāmātā, Lālbāī-Phūlbāī and Rogyādevī (for cure of diseases). The Bhīls call their lineage goddess *Ebrāmātā*. A temple in Ratlām tehsil in the district of the same name is where they make their offerings on the eighth day of *Kuār*

Navarātra. *Caitra Navarātra* is the largest festival in the Cāmuṇḍāmātā temple which they attend with the caste Hindus. They also worship Lord Śiva, but *bherū* is closer to them. Actually each caste has a lineage *bherū*. Gorā, Pātāl, Thokrā, Kālā, etc. are names of *bherū*. There is a saint of the *Śaiva* sect who is stationed at Cāmuṇḍāmātā temple and the villagers provide him with food and other necessary items. The villagers make offerings to Lord Śiva, Viṣṇu, Devīs, local deities and to local saints considered to be incarnations (Rāmdevabābā). The Jains participate and observe major Hindu festivals. The following is a list of rituals and festivals widely observed by some of the castes/communities in a calendar year. The Bhīls also observe these festivals. Mostly they prepare festive food items on such occasions.

Festival	*Mode of Observing the Festival*
Dhanteras	Important for Jains as they are in trade. Observed at the village level.
Dīwālī	Observed at the family level
Govardhan pūjā	Mainly celebrated by women.
Kārtik pūnam	People visit Ujjain and have *darśana* of Lord Mahākāl.
Til saṅkrānti	Observed by all at the family level.
Vasant pañcamī (Holī)	At the village level.
Śītalā saptamī	Observed at the family level. Offerings are made by women only.
Śivarātri	Observed in the houses; visits are made to Śiva temples and the Mahākāl temple at Ujjain.
Camuṇḍāmātā navrātra	At the *devī* temple.

Festival	*Mode of Observing the Festival*
Gaṅgore (*cait śukla tīja*)	Umā-Maheśa are worshipped. Attend the fair at Runija.
Rām navamī	At the village level.
Ākhātīja	Mainly by farmers.
Bherū pūjan	*Kula bherū pūjan* and *kul mātā pūjan*. Bherū is also worshipped on the eighth day of the bright half of Agahan (November-December) month.
Devāsā (*Śrāvaṇa*)	For the welfare and display, trade of livestock; at the village level.
Nāg pañcamī	At the village level; visits to Ujjain to have *darśana* of Nāgcandreśvar at the Mahākāl temple.
Rakṣā bandhana	Festival observed by all in the household. A section of the brahmans observe it as the day of renewal of the sacred thread.
Janmāṣṭamī	At the village level.
Ramdevajī pūjan (*Bhāḍon śukla dvītiyā*)	At the village level.
Ṛṣi pañcamī	Observed in the households as well as at village level.
Tejā daśamī (*Bhādon śukla daśamī*)	At the village level.
Ḍol egārās	At the village level.
Gajākiā (*Bhādon śukla bāras*)	Bhīla and Bhīlnī worshipped by caste Hindus at the village level.
Anant caudas	At the individual and household level.
Śrāddha pakṣa	For performing *śrāddha* some go to

Festival	*Mode of Observing the Festival*
	Rāmghāṭ at Ujjain. They make offerings to dead ancestors.
Sāñjhā pūjan	*Sāñjhā* is the worship of Devī by unmarried girls who ask for a good husband.
Navarātra	Mātā (*Kuladevī*) *pūjan* at the household level as well as village level.
Daśaharā	At the village level. The survivors of the *Jāgīrdār* cut the *śami* tree. The *śastras* (arms) are worshipped on this day by the traditional warrior castes. It is observed as Vijayā Daśamī, as on this day Lord Rāma killed demon king Rāvaṇa.

People here have visited Ujjain several times and performed the last rites at Rāmghāṭ and Sidhvaṭ. Brāhmaṇas of the village accompany them and guide them in the ritual. Actually these brāhmaṇas have contacts with particular *paṇḍās* at Ujjain and so take their *jajmāns* from the village to their *paṇḍā*. These brāhmaṇas get something from the *jajmāns* and also from the *paṇḍās*. There is a permanent relationship and interaction between some *paṇḍās* and these brāhmaṇas. A few wealthy farmers have *jajmānī* relations with *paṇḍās* at Ujjain. In general, the brāhmaṇas of the village mediate. *Sādhus* (saints) belonging to different *akhāḍās* at Ujjain pay regular visits to the village and there is no fixed date, time or person for this. Many villagers have participated in various *yātrās* at Ujjain and visited Ujjain during festivals. The Bhīls have also participated in *Pañcakośī yātrā* and *Somtī amāvasyā*, and attended various *melās* at Ujjain.

The village Jalwā is to the north of Ujjain. The Ujjain-Jhalawar road passes three kms away from the village. The village comes under the Ghattia block of Ujjain district.

In the village there are three important temples, two of which are very old. The temples of Lord Śiva and Kālikā *mātā* have very old construction. Bhagavatī temple is well-constructed. These temples face east and are near the *pañcāyat* office. In both of these *devī* temples (Bhagvatī and Kālikā), there are *Śivaliṅga*s and the images of *bherū*. Besides these, there are three temples dedicated to Lord Rāma and Kṛṣṇa. There are temples dedicated to Nāgadeva, *grām bherū, kheḍā bherū, kālā bherū, gorā bherū*, and Ājopāl or Pālyā. Here too, there are various lineage Bherū and lineage *mātā* who are worshipped on *bherū pūnam* and *Navarātra* respectively at the family level.

Some of the festivals and rituals observed at Jalwā in a year are given here alongwith some details.

Festival	*Mode of Observing the Festival*
Annakūṭa and Govardhan pūjā	At the village level.
Deva uṭhnī egāras	At the village level.
Kārtik melā	Attend fairs at Ujjain and have *darśana* of Lord Mahākāl in large numbers.
Til saṅkrānti	At the village level.
Pauṣ pūnam	Observed by unmarried girls.
Lāḍḍu cauth	At the village level.
Śivarātri	Observed at the village Śiva temple. Many go to Mahākāl temple at Ujjain to have *darśana* of Lord Mahākāl and make offerings.
Vasant pañcamī (Holī)	At the village level.
Lālbāī-Phūlbāī	At the village level.
Jāmrā or *Raṅga pañcamī*	At the village level.

Festival	Mode of Observing the Festival
Silisātam or *Sītā saptamī*	At the household level.
Cait navarātri	At the village temples. Also at the individual level.
Gaṅgor	At the village level.
Rām navamī	At the household level.
Pañcakośī yātrā	Wide participation at Ujjain. The villagers form a group.
Ākhātīja	Farmers at the village observe it as an auspicious day to start farming activities like ploughing.
Nirjalā ekādaśī	At the individual level.
Deva śayāni egāras	At the individual level.
Bherū pūnam	*Bherū* worshipped at family level.
Nāg pañcamī	At the village level. A number of villagers go to Ujjain to have *darśana* of Lord Nāg-candreśvar at the Mahākāl temple.
Rakṣābandhan	At the household level.
Śrāvaṇa Somvār	At the village level with fasts and offerings to Lord Śiva.
Śivarātri	At the village level. Several villagers go to the Mahākāl temple at Ujjain to make offerings.
Tījamātā pūjan (Bhādon kṛṣṇa tīja)	At the village level.
Hartālikā tīja (Bhādon śukla)	At the village level; worship of Śiva-Pārvatī by women.

Festival	Mode of Observing the Festival
Hal ṣaṣṭhī	At the household level.
Tejā daśamī	At the individual and household level.
Ḍol egāras	At the village level following the pattern that existed at Ujjain.
Anant caudas	At the individual level.
Śrāddha pakṣa	At the village level; sometimes go to Rāmghāṭ at Ujjain to perform *śrāddha* ritual.
Sāñjhā	*Sāñjhā* is the worship of Devī by unmarried girls for a good husband.
Navarātri	At the Bhagavatī temple.
Vijayā daśamī	At the village level.
Śarad pūnam	At the village level.

People here are well acquainted with the festivals observed at Ujjain. There is hardly anyone who has not seen the Mahākāl temple. They do not go to Ujjain for ritual performances, participation in *yātrā*s or *melā*s or for *darśana* of Mahākāleśvar only. They supply milk to various shops and purchase several necessary items. For the performance of the last rites they go to Sidhvaṭ and Rāmghāṭ. The village priest mediates and guides them in the performance of various rites. He earns from his *jajmān* and also gets a share of the amount given to the *paṇḍā* by his *jajmān*. Ujjain is the most sacred *tirtha* for the villagers and they participate in large numbers in various *yātrā*s like *Pañcakośī, Somti, Śani, Kārtik melā, Śivarātri, Siṁhastha*, etc. During the 1980 *siṁhastha mela*, they visited Ujjain several times. They were curious about the holy men who had gathered from all parts of the country. *Sādhu*s pay a visit to the village regularly.

Village Sirolyā presents more or less similar features. It is on the east of Ujjain and the nearest railway station is Maksi on the Ujjain-Bhopāl broad gauge link. It falls under Śājāpur district and is close to its border with Ujjain district. The Maksi-Guṇā railway line passes by the village. From Maksi it is about six kms and the villagers catch a bus for Ujjain at Maksi or go by train.

Here too there are a number of temples and the most important of these is Jharneśvar Mahādeva temple about half a kilometre away from the habitation area. There is a spring which has a perennial source of water, a big well and also a small tank under a mango grove. The temple has a *dharmaśālā*, which is quite popular in the area and people from distant places come here especially during fairs and for picnics as well. After taking a bath in the well water they prepare *dāl bāṭī*, a common food preparation in Mālwā and then make offerings to Lord Śiva. *Dāl bāṭī* is an essential offering in the *pūjan* of Lord Bherū. The waterhole here never dries up. The *Śivarātri* festival is observed with great enthusiasm and people from the neighbourhood come and make offerings to Lord Jharneśvar Mahādeva. It is considered as the Mahākāl of the neighbourhod and offerings to this temple make the people feel as if they are worshipping Lord Mahakal himself at Ujjain. At the temple there is a saint belonging to Junā *akhāḍā*, who stays here permanently. Two rooms are used by him — in one, he meditates and in the other, he gives *darśana* to others or discusses religious subjects. He also explains various things to the devotees and delivers lectures on special occasions. Besides this temple there are two temples of Lord Rāma, temple of Rāmdevabābā, a *Śivaliṅga*, a Lālbāī-Phūlbāī temple, a temple of Ājopāl, and a plate depicting *grām bherū*. There are several other *bherū* shrines and these are worshipped for various reasons: *Kheḍā bherū* for good crop, *grām bherū* for the protection of the villagers and *kula bherū* for the well-being of lineage members. Each caste group has its *bherū* and *mātā* who are worshipped in *bherū pūnam* and *Kūar navarātra* respectively by the family members. As said earlier, in *bherū pūjan*, '*dāl bāṭī*, or *baphlā*' is a must as *bhog*. Bheru worship does not always involve an image; it may involve worship of a couple of stones painted with vermilion mixed with oil. Anybody can make an offering to Lord Bherū. He is worshipped at individual, family and community levels. He is the protector and his blessings are gained to ensure a good crop. *Mātā* worship is next in importance to *bherū* worship.

Some of the festivals normally observed in village Sirolyā and some details on their observance are given below.

Festival	*Mode of Observing the Festival*
Dhanteras	At the village level; mainly observed by traders.
Rūpa caudas	At the village level.
Dīpāvalī	At the village level.
Annakūṭa and *Govardhan pūjā*	At the village level.
Deva uṭhni egāras	At the individual level.
Kārtik pūnam	Take a bath at various sacred tanks for the whole month. This bathing programme culminates with a bath in the holy Śiprā at Ujjain. At Ujjain they have *darśana* of Lord Mahākāl on this occasion and make offerings.
Āvlā navamī	In the village, a brāhmaṇa couple are fed.
Til saṅkrānti	At the village level.
Mahāśivarātri	At the Jharneśvar temple; many have *darśana* of Lord Mahākāl at Ujjain.
Holī	At the village level.
Śītalā saptamī	At the household level.
Daśamī (*cait kṛṣṇa*	At the village level; *Pīpal* tree *pūjan*

Festival	*Mode of Observing the Festival*
daśamī)	considering it as the seat of Lord Viṣṇu.
Gaṅgor	Śiva-Pārvatī *pūjan* at the village level.
Cait navarātra	Observed at the village level.
Akṣaya tṛtīyā	At the village level, mainly by farmers.
Deva śayanda egāras	At the individual level.
Bhairū pūnam	At the village level; involves *pūjan* of *kula bherū* and all the gods and
Festivals	*Details on Observing the festivals*
	goddesses of the village.
Haryālī amāvasyā	At the village level.
Nāg pañcamī	For *Nāg pañcamī* many go to Ujjain.
Rakṣābandhan	At the household level.
Janmāṣṭamī	At the village level.
Ḍol egāras	At the village level.
Anant caudas	In the villages, *Viṣṇu pūjan* and *Lālbāī-Phūlbāī pūjan* are performed.
Śrāddha pakṣa and *Sāñjhā*	Many go to Ujjain to perform *śrāddha*. Others observe *śrāddha* at Jharneśvar temple.
Kuār navrātra	At the village level. It involves *Kuladevī pūjan* or *Kula mātā pūjan*. It is observed as per *tithi* for each lineage. Some worship on the seventh or eighth day, while others do it on the sixth day. Accordingly, they say that they have *ātam mātā* or *sātam mātā* as their *kulamātā*.
Vijayā daśamī	Observed at the village level.

In various *yātrās* like *Pañcakośī, Cāradvāra, Aṣṭatīrthī, Somtī* or *Śani amāvasyā* the villagers participate in a group. Besides, they also participate in *Kārtik melā* at Ujjain. Ujjain is the most sacred place for them. For the performance of the last rites they feel that they do not need to go to Gayā or any other place because Ujjain is more sacred than these places. For a pilgrimage they start from Ujjain and end at Ujjain.

Ujjain provides a good market for milk and milk products. This village is a major supplier of milk and milk products to Ujjain. During visits to Ujjain, they always try to have *darśana* of Lord Mahākāl, at least from a distance.

The fourth village of our study is to the south of Ujjain. It is in the northernmost Sawar *tehsil* of Indore district. Kāṅkriyāpāl, the study village, is not far from Ujjain and the Indore-Ujjain meter-gauge link passes about three kms away from the village. The nearest railway station is Ājnoḍ. The villagers catch a bus for Ujjain from Sawar, the *tehsil* headquarters which is more than ten kms away from the village. There is, however, an all-weather road to Sawar.

Some of the rituals and festivals observed in this village in general have been cited here. The worship of caste deities has been kept out of our present consideration.

Festival	*Mode of Observing the Festival*
Dhanteras	Observed by the villages at the household and village level.
Rūpa caudas	At the village level.
Dīvālī	At the village level.
Annakūṭ and *Govardhan pūjā*	Observed at the village level.
Deva uṭhni egāras	At the individual level.

Festival	*Mode of Observing the Festival*
Kārtik pūnam	Attend *melā* at Ujjain in great numbers. Those who cannot go take a bath in the nearby auspicious well.
Til saṅkrānti	At the village as well as household level.
Mahāśivarātri	Observed at the Śiva temple in the village. Many go to Ujjain to make offerings to Lord Mahākāl.
Holī	At the hamlet-level and at the village level.
Raṅga pañcamī	At the village level.
Silisātan	At the household level
Gaṅgor (Cait śukla tīja)	At the village level; worship of Śiva Pārvatī by the women-folk.
Navrātri (Cait)	At the *Devī* temples in the village.
Rāmnavamī	At the household level and at the village level.
Ākhātīja or *Akṣaya tṛtīyā*	By the farmers at the village level.
Devason egāras	At the individual level.
Bherū Pūnam	Worship of *kula bherū* and the gods and goddesses of the village.
Haryālī amāvasyā	At the village level.
Śrāvaṇa somvār	Offerings made at Śiva temples in the village; many go to attend the last *somvār savārī* of Mahākāl at Ujjain.
Nāg pañcamī	At the village level by making offerings. Many go to Ujjain.

Festival	Mode of Observing the Festival
Rakṣā bandhan	At the household level.
Tejā daśamī	At the village and household level.
Janmāṣṭamī	At the village level.
Ḍol egāras	At the Viṣṇu temples of the village.
Merī mātā pūjan (*Bhādon amāvasyā*)	At the village by Paṭel and Balai for the protection of the villagers.
Śrāddha pakṣa and *Sāñjhā*	People also go to Ujjain for *śrāddha* (ancestor worship) performance. Unmarried girls worship Devī Pārvatī for a good husband. Observed at the household level.
Kuār navarātra	It involves *Kuladevī* or *Kulamātā pūjan* as per the *tithi*, like *saptamī*, *aṣṭamī*, etc. Observed at the household level as well as at the village level.
Daśaharā	At the village level.

Each family has a *kula bherū* and *kula devī* or *kula mātā*. The former is worshipped on *bherū pūnam* (*Āsaḍha*) day and the latter is worshipped during *Kuār navarātra* by the family members. In *bherū pūjan, dāl bāṭī* or *dāl bāphlā* as an offering is a must. There is a collection of red painted stones known by the name of different *bherū*. In the village there is a *devī* temple, a temple dedicated to Tejājī and Rāmdevabābā and another to Lord Rāma. The Devī temple is quite big and faces west. A large *Śivaliṅga* is found inside. The Devī is popularly known as Bhagavatī. There was no resident saint during our visit. This village is, however, on the route taken by the saints collecting a subscription for a *Śaiva* (Dattā) *akhāḍa* of Ujjain. The saints come for subscription announcing their arrival with a *jai mahākāl* in loud tones at the doors of the villagers whom they identify with clean castes. The household members offer cereals. Besides, there are two saints of the *Śaiva* sect who come regularly (once in a week) for *Madhukarī* (begging for saints). They sit for a while and talk on various subjects relating to rituals and the villagers patronise these saints considering it a holy act.

In *Pañcakośī yātrā* and other *yātrās* like *somtī* and *śani amāvasyā* and *Kārtik melā*, the villagers visit Ujjain in large numbers. For the performance of the last rites, they go to Ujjain with the help of the village priest. During *siṁhastha* (1980), a large contingent of them visited Ujjain. There is hardly any adult who has not visited Ujjain or has not had *darśana* of Lord Mahākāl on some occasion or the other.

Through Folk Theatre

Māch is the folk theatre of Mālwā and a well-recognised folk theatre of India. It is believed to have derived its name from *mañca* or stage. The tradition of *Māch* most probably started in the early part of the eighteenth century. Paṇḍit Sūryanārāyaṇa Vyās has tried to establish the relations of *Māch* with *Bhān* dramas of the Gupta period (Guptakālīna Śṛṅgārhāṭ — Vyās). Raghubir Singh is in favour of linking this with *khyāl*, the popular folk drama of Mewār. In the language of the *Māch* dramas there is a direct influence of Mewārī. Mālvī is the main language used as media but there are many Mewārī words also. *Māch* has taken various aspects from other traditions such as acting from *dhārā-dhārī*, song from *turrā-kalaṅgī*, joking and amusement from *swānga nakal*.

Ujjain is the place where *Māch* has taken its form, developed, and become popular. The present form of this folk theatre owes its origin to this holy city. Till date, the most popular *Māch* troupes, ranging from most traditional to modernised, hail from Ujjain. All the *Māch gūrūs* (teachers) are from Ujjain and the city has the highest number of troupes. They stage dramas in the rural areas and their patrons are mainly from these areas.

The ruling deity of *Māch* is Bherū or Bhairava or Bhairavanāth. Ritual performances are related to *Māch*, particularly with the *mañca* or stage. All the actors pay respect (by bowing down) before entering the stage. The construction of the stage is ritually started a fortnight earlier and *tāntrika* influence is observable here too. In each drama troupe normally there is a *Nāth-yogī*. The *Nāth-yogī*s were *tāntrika*s and come under the *Śaiva* sect. Ujjain is traditionally a great centre of the *Nāth-yogī*s. King Bhartṛhari (elder brother of the legendary King Vikramāditya) became one of the nine principal *Nāth*s of the *Nāth sampradāya*. Lord Śiva is their prime god, but they are different from the *Daśanāmī*s. There are many *Nāth akhāḍās* (centres) and temples under the control of the *Nāth*s at Ujjain. This sect has influenced the *Māch* tradition to a great extent.

Bhairava vandanā (prayer) is a must for staging any *Māch* drama. *Bhavānī vandanā* and *Gaṇapati vandanā* are also performed since they are essential. Finally they pray to Lord Mahākāl. The *Māch* dramas are based mainly on stories from the *Purāṇa*s, the historical character of love stories or on religious subjects. The themes of some of the recent dramas are new and related to present-day incidents.

This folk theatre is a medium that has a strong influence on the village. Besides, the professionals such as *kathāvācak*, *ācārya* and those who read the religious texts explain the inner themes. This way the message is carried to the illiterate masses. This medium propagates the holiness of Ujjain and the greatness of Lord Mahākāl.

6

The City of Trade

I

AVANTIKĀ was a knot in the ancient trade routes of India. The routes from south to north and east to west traversed this city. The route connecting the towns of Punjab plains and Gujarāt passed through this city. One of the link roads was through Bhṛgukacch (Bharoch). Another link of the southern highway was through Bhṛgūkacch and Supārik (Sopārā) port which reached Kauśāmbī through the Betoa hill terrains. From Mathurā there was a link road to Ujjain through the Chambal tract which reached Māhiṣmatī (Maheśvar) on the bank of Narmadā. The traders of Tamil Nadu reached Kāśī via Ujjain. It had trade links with Kauśāmbī, Kāśī and Pampā on the east. Ports of the Gujarāt coast were important trade centres. Ancient India had trade relations with Persia and Arabia. Ujjain was the route to the Gujarat coast for the trade centres of the east like Magadha, Pāṭaliputra and Kāśī. During the Mauryan period Ujjain was a busy trade centre dealing in diamonds, rubies and other precious stones, gold and conch-shells.

The Gujarāt ports gradually lost their importance and with the fall of Magadha, the cities of the east no longer remained centres of trade. Before this, Ujjain was a flourishing city of wealthy people. During the later Muslim rule in India the rulers secured land routes through the north-western front, and so the Gujarāt ports lost their grandeur.

Actually Ujjain retained its status as the main trade centre of Mālwā even after the fall of the Mauryan empire. It was the capital of Mālwā. During the Paramāra rule and under some Muslim rulers, the capital was shifted to Dhār and Māṇḍu. But these places could not develop as stable urban centres. Vidiśā for some time became prominent as a trade centre. But it did not affect the growth of Ujjain, because Vidiśā is on the eastern fringe of Mālwā. During Marāṭhā rule, Ujjain again came into prominence.

The growth of Indore and the fact of it emerging as an industrialised city posed a great threat to Ujjain. But, in Ujjain, a centralised industrial set-up came into existence with the establishment of two cotton mills. A rayon yarn factory and, very recently, a tube factory have also come up. Ujjain, however, trails far behind Indore as an industrialised city. Indore is the most industrialised city of Mālwā, and it is the largest centre of capital trade. The emergence of Nāgdā as a Birlā township, which has a large population attached to industry, has also affected the status of Ujjain. The advantage of Indore is its location on the Bombay-Delhi highway and its link with Calcutta, Delhi and Madras through the broad-gauge railroad. To a large extent, it is the growth of Indore that has hindered the growth of Ujjain. In centralised trade Ujjain is the second city of Mālwā. The two cities are not far and there is a regular bus service connecting the two.

Ujjain, however, retains its monopoly in certain trades and these are mostly related to sacred performances. Its status as a pilgrim centre has given rise to the construction of various temples. The materials used for daily rituals and those performed by pilgrims — ritual items like *dhūp, agarbattī, kumkum, candan, mehandī, gulāl, abīr, saubhāgya upakaran sut, lacha, āsan,* sacred thread, *itra, gūlābjal,* flower and milk products — have a good market in this holy city as well as in other areas. A considerable amount of the total product is transported to the towns and villages of Mālwā and elsewhere. Some of these trades may be discussed here in brief.

II

Agarbattī and Dhūpbattī

There are two big workshops which provide employment to more than three hundred persons. *Gūgal, candan, lobān,* meda stick, coal dust, *maśālā* powder and bamboo sticks are the raw materials used. There is a caste named Bansford that prepares the sticks for the purpose. The items have a good market here and outside. Packing, labelling, etc. are done mainly by women labourers. *Candan agarbattī* is considered the favourite of Lord Kṛṣṇa and Śiva and *Gūgal agarbattī* is the favourite of mother goddess (Devī). *Lobān agarbattī* is not used by the Hindus. *Dhūpbattī* is thick like a cigarette and dark in colour. The special type of wood required is acquired from Amritsar in Punjab. Daily production is as much as ten gross and each gross consists of one hundred and forty-four packets, while each packet carries eight sticks. Ujjain *agarbattīs* are preferred and sold at a higher price than other brands.

Bilva Patra, Tulasī and Flowers

There is a permanent market in Malipura area near the railway station and central bus stand dealing in these commodities. In this market there are as many as twenty-seven permanent shops selling these items. Mālī (*phūlamālī*) caste people are horticulturists by tradition. They have been in this trade for long. These shops sell the articles in front of many temples as well to meet the needs of the devotees. There is a caste known as Bhoi which was originally a fishing community. They used to catch fish in minor tributaries and in the river Śiprā. Fishing was not a profitable enterprise, and so probably many of them have switched to other occupations such as supplying *bilva patra* and *tulasī* to the shops and temples. *Bilva patra* is a must for Śiva-worship and similarly without *tulasī patra* the worship of Lord Viṣṇu or his incarnations is considered incomplete. Besides, people here have some idols in their houses and performing *pūjan* in the morning is part of their daily routine. After taking a bath they perform the *pūjan* and then have their food or go to work. The Bhoi people maintain a house-to-house supply service of packets containing flowers, *bilva patra* and *tulasī*. They do it on monthly payment and the shopkeepers also employ persons for this purpose. Mainly *sevantī, gandhā, gūlāb, pārad, kuṇḍa, camelī, jūthicā, cāndnī, mogrā, nivārī, kesar, revatī, bijlī, navraṅga* and *sūryamukhī* are the varieties of flowers grown. There are persons specialised in making flower garlands, flower ornaments and flower arrangements, bouquets, etc. There is a lucrative market for these commodities at Ujjain and Indore, Bhopāl, Dhār and other towns of the neighbourhood.

Oil extracted from *camelī* is one of the important materials used for *śṛṅgāra*. Making a paste by mixing *kumkum* and *camelī* oil and painting the stones and idols with this is the most popular way of *śṛṅgāra* (make-up). *Camelī* oil is widely used and produced for commercial purposes.

Raṅgīna-nāḍā (Coloured Thread)

This is used in almost all kinds of worship. The *jajmān* and *purohit* are bound to each other with this holy thread at the time of some ritual performances. It also serves as a substitute *dhotī* for the poor *jajmāns* while they make offerings to various deities. There is a couplet highlighting the phenomena, *yenā tvām rakṣamānāhi rakṣāngmā calsmācal*. It is used in *Rakṣābandhan, kathā, abhiṣeka* and other ritual performances. Thread, colour, soda, soap and alum are the raw materials used. The product has a good market in rural and urban Mālwā as well as outside. Ujjain *nāḍās* have not only technical superiority but a great sacred value attached to it. Sacred threads are also prepared on a large scale. After various ritual performances the sacred thread is changed and such rituals are quite common. These threads are produced in cottage industries.

Kumkum is used for perfoming *śṛṅgāra* of idols. It is produced on a large scale. It has a market not only in Ujjain but in the neighbouring towns also. Besides, putting a *tilak* mark on the forehead is expected of a Hindu. The form of *tilak* distinguishes the saints and commoners, their affiliation to different *akhāḍā*s and sects. It is a must for the ascetics. There are eighteen centres producing *kumkum*. Lemon, colour, turmeric and alum are the raw materials used. *Kumkum* of red, blue, yellow, orange and green colours are produced. Red is used for ritual purposes. There is a tradition of making *māṇḍnā* (floor arts) on the eve of various festivals or occasions and there is a specific design popular as Mālvī design. This is done with various colours of *kumkum*. *Mehandī* is also produced on a large scale and has a good market outside.

Stone images of various gods and goddesses such as *Śivaliṅga*, *yantras*, *mālā*s (necklace) of *rudrākṣa* or *tulasī* wood, etc. are other ritual materials that have a good market here. The pilgrims also do some shopping and these things fascinate them the most. Members of a caste known as Silavat are traditionally efficient in stone carvings. They are originally from Rājasthān and have settled here for a good living. They also do it in front of the customers to attract them. Wooden plaques depicting various gods and goddesses are widely sold. *Rudrākṣamālā* is the favourite of Lord Śiva and his followers while *mālā* of *tulasī* wood is favoured by Lord Viṣṇu and his devotees. Both the things are sold in large quantities. *Mālā* made of lotus seeds also has a good market. There were several sacred lakes in Avantikā and these were in good condition, with lotuses blooming in them. Wearing *mālā*s of lotus seeds is very common here and they are available in plenty.

In *naivedya* (food offerings) for the *pūjan* of the various deities, sweets are used. The type of sweet varies according to the season and type of ritual performed. *Māvā* is the raw material for the various and it comes from the villages of the neighbourhood. Milk and milk products are consumed in substantial quantities and also sold in the markets of other towns. Ujjain *peḍā* has a good customer base. The visitors favour these delicious products and also carry them back to their native places. A number of people are engaged in various stages of this trade from raising calves to selling sweets.

The most important trade of Ujjain is perhaps the 'sacred trade' or trade in sacred performances that involves earning from temples or through some priestly services. In this trade, mostly the brāhmaṇa professionals earn from the pilgrims and other visitors. It is their caste identity that helps them to earn their bread. Sometimes the pilgrims are caught unawares and made to part with some amount though this happens rarely.

Snān or taking a bath is one of the most auspicious performances at *tīrthas* and *kṣetras*. Ujjain is both a *tīrtha* and a *kṣetra*. There are various types of *snān* prescribed in the sacred texts. Of these, two are most important — *bhasmasnān* or *agnisnān* and *jalasnān* or *varuṇasnān*. *Jalasnān* is widely practised. After *snān*, *dāna* is a must which varies according to *tithi*, etc. And giving *dāna* to brāhmaṇas is to earn *puṇya*. The brāhmaṇas are the sellers of *puṇya* and they have the right to oblige the devotees by accepting *dāna*. Besides, there is the tradition of brāhmaṇa *bhojana* (giving a feast to brāhmaṇas) in which brāhmaṇas are requested to come and have the meal. After that *dakṣiṇā* is given to the brāhmaṇa. Brāhmaṇas bless and ask for an amount for the blessing that has been conferred.

There are several ways of selling *puṇya* and offering protection from ill-fate. At the *ghāṭs* in the role of *tīrtha pūrohits*, the brāhmaṇas offer some specific services. They perform various rites like mortuary rites and those performed before and after a pilgrimage. The *jajmān* has to pay dearly for the same. Besides, they put the *ṭikā* mark on the forehead or give blessings to the devotees and expect some amount. At the *ghāṭ*s there are some temples that are uncared for and neglected. Brāhmaṇas who come to Ujjain to earn select some open space and sit there with *pūjan* articles or clean an uncared-for temple and start making offerings. They sit there reading the sacred texts while the visitors leave some coins at the temple. Thus they start earning. Some kinship link with the brāhmaṇa professionals of Ujjain helps a lot in these ventures.

For the performance of a ritual or a *pūjan* at the temple, the *pujārī* or *paṇḍā* charges some amount. They always try to make it very attractive to gain the confidence of the *jajmān*. Their interaction with the *jajmān*s varies with the economic and social status of the *jajmān*. So the brāhmaṇa first tries to find a temple where he can begin and earns by performing the *pūjan*s for the devotees. Some share of the earning is given to the chief priest of this temple. Sometimes the professionals select some neglected temple. Then they perform *abhikṣeka*, *pūjan* or organise a *yajña* to draw the attention of the devotees. Then some *camatkār* (magic or wonder) is announced and finally some myth linked to the gods and goddesses of the Hindu pantheon is created. Modern media like the newspaper is also used to publicise the performance in the temple to attract the devotees. This way the temple flourishes and becomes a source of earning for the brāhmaṇa professionals.

Constructing a temple is a common thing here. But the temples are constructed along the route of the devotees' movement like from the Rāmghāṭ to Mahākāl temple, or near a famous temple or already popular temple. If we look into the distribution of temples in Ujjain, there is a concentration of temples along the river Śiprā and in the old city area towards the southern part. Besides, there are some complexes like Maṅgalnāth, Sidhvaṭ and

Aṅkpaṭ. Mostly temples come up in these areas of concentration (Mahākāl to Gopāl Mandir zone). The reason is that the devotees while making offerings at one temple also give some amount as *praṇāmī* at the neighbouring temples which fall in their route. It has been found that at some places the section of the front room or portion of the house has been transformed into a temple. An image is installed and the visiting devotees passing by it leave some coins. Temples are constructed near a temple which is already popular, since the popular temple attracts the pilgrims. While performing some ritual at the popular temple they also make some offerings at the new temples. The *pūjārī* of the main temple does not object because the professional and caste affinity works and also, as he gets some portion of the earning. An increase in the number of temples increases the area of the complex as also its popularity. A complex attracts more people and fetches more money than a lone temple. So we find various clusters have come up at Ujjain. Temple construction is also profitable to exploit the psychic need towards religious observances. For instance, in a newly-constructed colony there were no temples. But then a resident converted one of his front rooms into a Śiva temple. It was a single-floor, small house. He was a brāhmaṇa by caste and the temple was kept open for the residents of the colony. The residents, to satisfy their religious need and for convenience, started making offerings in this temple. Gradually it became the most popular temple of that sector. The owner of the house has extended it further and it has become one of the important sources of income for his family. Such cases are also seen in some other newly-developed colonies. In course of time these temples get linked to some myths to gain popularity. Giving *caraṇāmṛta, prasāda, ṭikā* or *aratī* are other sources of income. Thugh this service is given without any claim the popular practice is to pay some amount. Some characteristics are added to the image of the temple to make its identity separate from others. This is also to draw the attention of the devotees (like in the case of the Baḍāgaṇeśa or Bṛhat Hanumān temple).

The other interesting point is that the temple clusters are heterogeneous with regard to temples dedicated to gods and goddesses. In a cluster there are temples dedicated to various gods. For example, in the Mahākāl complex, besides various *Śivaliṅga*s and Śiva temples, there are temples dedicated to Gaṇapati, Hanumān, Narasiṁha, Sākṣīgopāl, Pāṇḍharīnāth, Rām-Jānakī, Navagraha, Khāṇḍobā, eleven *jyotirliṅga*, eighty-four *liṅga*s, etc. This provides an opportunity to the devotees belonging to various sects to make offerings. For Gāṇapatyas there is Gaṇapati temple, for Vaiṣṇavites there are Viṣṇu temples and so on. One can have the *puṇya* of visiting twelve *jyotirliṅga*s by making offerings to Ekādaśa liṅgeśvar and Mahākāl or can avoid visiting all the eighty-four sacred *liṅga*s spread over the whole city by making offerings to Caurāsī Liṅgeśvar. Another reason for this is perhaps to draw people from various sects. If a man owns four temples, he earns more in normal cases than one who has one temple. The devotees while making some cash offering to one temple hardly ignore any others in the neighbourhood or those that fall on their route. They may pay small amounts but do not avoid the temple. During big fairs it is always profitable to own more temples. This also helps in managing the devotees willing to make offerings on such occasions. There are shops who supply change for currency notes of higher denominations to the devotees on commission. The *pujārī* insists that the devotee give some amount to all the deities which he collects afterwards.

There is another way of earning for the brāhmaṇas. They do *pārāyaṇa* (repeatedly reading some sacred book) or read and explain sacred texts (*kathāvācaka*) or deliver lectures on religious philosophies (*pravacana*) and also perform *jāpa* (repeating a god's name for a period of time) and other rituals as desired by the devotees on payment. They do this at specific temples. The priests also perform *yajña*s and other rituals on payment. Elaboration of the performances depends upon the amount of money the devotee is ready to spend. For instance, in case of a *laghurudra* one has to pay rupees one hundred and twenty one while for *mahārūdrābhiṣeka* one has to pay more than rupees one thousand.

7

Śiva-Worship in Mālwā

I

THE temple of Lord Mahākāleśvar is not only the main temple of Ujjain but also the most popular Śiva temple in Mālwā. As said earlier, it is one of the twelve *jyotirliṅgas* in the country. These *jyotirliṅgas* are distributed in different parts of India, but they are mainly concentrated in central India. These are believed to be self-effulgent *liṅgas*. The twelve *jyotirliṅgas* are as follows.

Name	*Distance from Ujjain*	*Location*
Śrī Somnāth	860 kms	Prabhas Pattan (Gujarāt)
Śrī Mallikārjuna	1652 kms	Shailam Hill of Andhra Pradesh
Śrī Mahākāleśvar		Ujjain
Śrī Māmleśvar Oṁkāreśvar	152 kms	Oṁkāreśvar (Madhya Pradesh)
Śrī Baidanāth	1164 kms	Pasli Railway Station (Mahārāṣṭra)

Name	*Distance from Ujjain*	*Location*
Śrī Bhimaśaṅkara	986 kms	Near Railway Station Bombay-Pune railroad (Mahārāṣṭra)
Śrī Rāmeśvar	2290 kms	Rameśvaram (Tamil Nadu)
Śrī Nāgesvar	626 kms	In Abda village of Parbhani district, near Hingoli Railway Station (Mahārāṣṭra)
Śrī Viśvanātha	1030 kms	Vārāṇasī
Śrī Trayambakeśvar	609 kms	Nāsik (twelve miles from Nāsik station).
Śrī Kedārnātha	1262 kms	Kedārnātha (Uttar Pradesh)
Śrī Ghisneśvar	657 kms	In Verul village, twenty-two miles from Auraṅgābāda (Mahārāṣṭra).

There are differences of opinion about the claim of some of these temples as *jyotirliṅgas*, like the Baidyanāth temple. There is a temple of Baidyanāth in Bihār which is more popular. Mention of these *jyotirliṅgas* is there in various *Purāṇas* and other writings. Here we find that except the four *jyotirliṅgas* in four directions of the country, the rest are located in central India.

Oṁkāreśvar is located on the bank of river Narmadā in

Khaṇḍvā district of Madhya Pradesh and it is the other *jyotirliṅga* in Mālwā. Oṁkāreśvar, in importance as a place of Śiva-worship in Mālwā, is next only to Ujjain. There are a number of Śiva temples on the bank of the holy river Narmadā. A number of *dharmaśālās* are there to accommodate the pilgrims during festivals. It attracts people mainly from the tribal belt and rural Mālwā. The Korku of Dewās and Khaṇḍvā districts and other neighbouring areas believe that they have been created by Lord Śiva and are also protected by him. The Pañcamārī Mahādeva temple of Chindwārā district was under the control of *Korku jāgīrdārs*. It is extremely popular not only among the Korku but also among other tribal groups like some sections of Goṇḍs and Bhīla. On the *Śivarātri* day, tribals from Mahārāṣṭra also visit this temple and make offerings to Lord Śiva. There is a festival of *Mahādeva vivāha* (marriage of Lord Śiva) which is in reality enacted by the members of the Korku and Goṇḍ tribes. Oṁkāreśvar temple is also held in high esteem among the tribals of southern and western Mālwā.

There is special link between Lord Mahākāleśvar and Lord Oṁkāreśvar. At the Mahākāleśvar temple the *liṅga* of Lord Oṁkāreśvar is located in the chamber right above that of Lord Mahākāleśvar. In Oṁkāreśvar temple on the Narmadā bank the arrangement is the reverse. The devotee visiting either of the temples becomes aware of the other *jyotirliṅga* in Mālwā. Again the *paṇḍās* and *pujāris* talk of the greatness of the other temple and advise the devotees to pay their *darśana* there as well. The *paṇḍās* and *pujāris* of one temple are respected by those of the other temple and are given special treatment. Such a link is not to be seen in the case of the other *jyotirliṅgas*. Both of these temples have pilgrims mainly from Mālwā. Ujjain attracts people from a wider area for other considerations like *siṁhastha mela*, etc.

At Oṁkāreśvar there are branches of several *akhāḍās* which have their units at Ujjain also. The *akhāḍās* maintain links between these two places of pilgrimage. Besides, visiting saints and ascetics keep the atmosphere religious at both the places. They are the elements who maintain a strong link between these two pilgrim centres of Mālwā and their link with the sacred *kṣetras* in other parts of the country. Their countrywide network of centres in almost all the major pilgrim centres also helps to maintain some common characteristics by way of a uniform life-style and activities. Besides, they keep the tradition alive in these centres of gods and godmen.

III

Besides these there are other centres of Śiva-worship in Mālwā. Next in importance to these two *jyotirliṅgas* is Maheśvar. Maheśvar of today was the ancient Māhiṣmatī of the days of the great epics. It is said that with the fall of Māhiṣmatī as a centre of political power, Ujjain came into prominence as the political centre of Mālwā. Maheśvar is situated on the north bank of the river Narmadā, the most sacred river of central India, near the confluence of the river Maheśvar and Narmadā. The name of the city implies a link with Lord Śiva. It is said that a king by the name of Maheśvar had Lord Śiva as his tutelary deity. So he named this city which was the capital of his kingdom after his beloved Lord. King Māhiṣmān of the Haihaya dynasty renamed it as Māhiṣmatī. In later years the old name was revived and Māhiṣmatī became Maheśvar. It was a trade centre and the ancient Indian trade route from Tamil Nadu to Kāśī passed through it. The pilgrims and traders used to go to Kāśī or Pāṭaliputra via Māhiṣmatī, Avantikā and Vidiśā. There was a direct road from Māhiṣmatī to Ujjain. The two pilgrim centres as well as trade and political centres have age-old links.

According to various *Purāṇas* and the great epics, the Haihaya King Sahasrajit or Kārtavīryārjuna was a mighty ruler and a great warrior. Māhiṣmatī was his capital city. With the fall of Ayodhyā, the Haihayas extended their territory to the north and became the principal power in Āryāvarta. Kārtavīryārjuna was a character in the *Rāmāyaṇa* who defeated King Rāvaṇa. The Haihayas practically drove away the Karkoṭaka Nāga, the original settlers of the area. There are many things that are associated with this powerful king. Sahasradhārā is one such thing attributed to this legendary king. He was a worshipper of Lord Śiva. The tutelary deity of Maheśvar is also Lord Śiva, like that of Ujjain and Oṁkāreśvar. During the reign of Kārtavīryārjuna, Māhiṣmatī reached its zenith. It is said that King Kārtavīrya was defeated and killed by the brāhmaṇa warrior, Paraśūrāma. And the downfall of Māhiṣmatī followed. Actually King Kārtavīrya shifted the capital from Mahidpura in Ujjain district to Maheśvar. In the *Mahābhārata* war, the King of Mahiṣmatī took the side of the Kauravas like the princes of Avantikā.

All through the ages there have been a number of Śiva temples at Maheśvar and Śiva-worship persisted. Maheśvar's location on the bank of the sacred river Narmadā has given it a high status as a sacred centre. River Narmadā is believed to be as sacred as the Gaṅges. It is equally sacred for the performance of last rites. The belief is, once the last remains of the deceased after cremation is immersed in Narmadā waters, it takes the form of a *liṅga* in course of time. And the soul becomes free from the cycle of rebirth. *Liṅga*-shaped stones are found in plenty near Oṁkāreśvar and Maheśvar.

During the Muslim rule Maheśvar remained neglected by various dynasties. With the sanction of the Peśavā, in 1734, Malhārarāo Holkar, one of the powerful *sardārs* of the Marāṭhā confederacy, founded his *jāgīr* at Maheśvar. Initially it consisted of nine villages from Indore district with the capital at Maheśvar. During the Holkar rule, there was all-round development in Maheśvar. Many temples were renovated and constructed, and an elaborate town planning was laid. Renovation and reconstruction of temples and *ghāṭs* to revive the honour of the Hindu pilgrim centre is a policy that has come to be associated with Marāṭhā rulers of the country. Maheśvar flourished under royal patronage. It received additional care at the time of Ahilyābāī Holkar, the queen of Holkar state. It was due to her initiative that various temples came up at Maheśvar. She was the third successor of the Holkar State. Following the treaty of Mandasaur, the capital of the state was shifted from Maheśvar. Malhārarāo II of the Holkars founded the new capital at Indore on the bank of river Khan. This hindered the growth of Maheśvar and Indore was made capital in the year 1818. Though Maheśvar lost its political importance, it has retained its sacred status till today. It attracts people from rural Malwā in large numbers. Direct bus routes link Ujjain and Oṁkāreśvar to Maheśvar and Maṇḍaleśvar. Maṇḍaleśvar is about five kms away from Maheśvar. There are many Śiva temples in Maheśvar. People come to Maheśvar and Maṇḍaleśvar on pilgrimage. Special buses ply during a fair or festival of Lord Śiva.

Mandasaur, the district town north of Ujjain, is famous for the temple of Paśupatināth. It is a Śiva temple, the *liṅga* having four faces. This *liṅga* is an imitation of that of the original Paśupatināth temple in Kāṭhmāṇḍu. People take the holy dip in the nearby sacred lake on the eve of the *melā* and make offerings to Lord Paśupatināth. It attracts devotees from various places including Rājasthān. Similarly, Gotampurā on the bank of the river Carmanvatī or Cambal is a historically important place. There is a huge and famous temple dedicated to Lord Śiva. A *melā* is observed every year. It is in the district of Ujjain. Gotampurā attracts people from the rural areas of Mālwā. The present-day bustling city of Indore was a small village in the eighteenth century on the bank of river Khan. It derives its name from the ruling deity, Indreśvar Mahādeva. There is a temple of Lord Śiva heɪe. Indore was the halt when travelling from south to north. The Indreśvar temple used to attract people from the rural areas of Mālwā. The Holkars and Scindias have renovated and constructed various Śiva temples at Maheśvar and Ujjain respectively. They have constructed *ghāṭ*s at Vārāṇasī too. The Scindias who had Dwārkādhiśa as their family deity, brought back the ancient honour of the pilgrim centre to Ujjain. Even where the memorials of the members of royalty at Indore (Holkar) and Ujjain (Scindia) are concerned, a *Śivaliṅga* has been installed at every memorial. This is a local tradition particularly practised by the ascetics.

Besides these, the Śiva temples of Māhidpur, Tārana, Śājāpur, Dewās, and Dhār are fairly popular. The first three are on the bank of minor streams and during scheduled fairs people from rural Mālwā come and make offerings to Lord Śiva. These fairs are mostly held one after the other so that traders can conveniently attend most of them. There is a temple constructed by a British officer posted at the place.

The Śiva temples in Mālwā have some characteristic features. The temple normally faces east having a conical dome. The dome has *mañjarīs* (cones) or rows of *kalaśa* (pots) or both. At the temple top there is a coconut (of stone) placed on the *maṅgal kalaśa* (pot) with a *jhaṇḍā* (flag) usually of *bhagvā* (yellow) colour and projecting *triśūla* (trident) upwards. Normally the temples are made of stone (dark basalt rock). It has three parts — *sabhāmaṇḍapa*, the *garbhagṛha* and a space between them. *Sabhāgṛha* has rows of pillars in big temples while in small temples there are only a few pillars. The space between the *sabhāmaṇḍapa* and *garbhagṛha* houses the Nandī, directly related to Lord Śiva, who guards the entry. On wall shelves on the two sides the images of Pārvatī and Kārtik are kept. Lord Gaṇapati is there on the centre of the upper beam of the door frame. The *garbhagṛha* is at a lower level than the *sabhāmaṇḍapa* and the space between them. It is always below the surface level. In the temples which are constructed at a higher level than the surface, to keep with the tradition, inside the *garbhagṛha* is the *Śivaliṅga* with the *jaladhārī* or Viṣṇuyoni. The *jaladhārī* is towards the north. It also shows the direction to strangers. The images of Gaṇapati, Pārvatī and Kārtik Svāmī are on the south, west and north wall shelves respectively. The Śiva temples always house the *Pañcadevatā* — (Gaṇapati, Pārvatī, Kārtik Svāmī), Lord Śiva or Śivaliṅga and Nandī. The *abhiṣekpātra* suspends right above the *liṅga*. It has a pore at the base and it is kept filled with water. This is to maintain constant dropping of water over the *liṅga*. The ceiling has the sacred *aṣṭakoṇa* (eight-angled). Sometimes all these characteristics may not be found in some temples. But this is the general pattern observed in Mālwā. The Mahākāl temple has many uncommon things which have been mentioned earlier. This is because it is the most important Śiva temple of Mālwā. The ladies here neither touch Lord Kārtik Svāmī, nor do they make any offerings. It is believed that if they do so, they will have to face widowhood.

There is hardly any village that lacks a place of Śiva-worship. A temple or a *liṅga* in other temples or on a raised platform serve the purpose. So we find Śiva temples at three levels — at the village, at the neighbourhood and at the sub-regional level. The temples or *liṅgas* in the remote villages are for the villagers at large. Śiva temples of Mandasaur, Tārana, Indore, etc. attract people of the neighbourhood. Maheśvar, Maṇḍaleśvar and Oṁkāreśvar attract devotees from the rural as well as urban areas of Mālwā. Oṁkāreśvar and Mahākāleśvar are pilgrim centres where people come from distant places of the country.

In Mālwā villages, two folk deities are very popular and important, and these are Bhairava and *mātā*. The Bhairavas are always there in any *devī* temple. Bhairavas are of various kinds and are used for various purposes. They are worshipped at the lineage level, personal level and village level. This worship is equally popular among the castes and the tribes. The Bhairava is identified with Lord Śiva and they who serve him are believed to be his creation. Kālabhairava and Gorābhairava are the two principal Bhairavas worshipped in Mālwā. There are temples dedicated to them at Ujjain. The Kālabhairava temple at Bhairugaḍh on the west bank of Śiprā and Gorābhairava temple on the other bank of the river in Rājmalghāt (crematorium) are very important. *Dāl-bāṭī* or *dāl-bāphlā*, which are the most common food items of Mālwā, are seen as a must for *naivedya* for Lord Bhairū or Bhairava. In Bhairū-worship, there are *pañca-makārs* (five ingredients — *mad, māna, macchī, mātsarya* and *maithuna*). *Yoni mudrā* is shown after *pūjan* and this is a *tāntrika* tradition that still exists. Bhairava is believed to be an angry deity who also protects his followers. Kālabhairava is a more powerful and angry deity than Gorābhairava. Rudrarūpa has been assigned to Lord Bhairū. In most places in the villages there is no temple of Bhairū but mostly shrines consisting of red painted stones. The dog is the companion of Lord Bherū and so it is blessed by him. People avoid beating dogs as this way they may earn the curse or wrath of the deity. Bherū is a part of their life in rural Mālwā. Not only is he worshipped at lineage or village level for protection but he is also the deity of the folk drama *Māch*. There are *gotra bherū, grām bherū, kheḍā bherū* and the like. As *gotra bherū* he protects the family members and maintains the identity of the lineage. As *kheḍā bherū*, he is responsible for a good harvest and as *grām bherū* he is the protector of the village.

The other important deity is *mātā*, the mother goddess. She is identified with Pārvatī, the consort of Lord Śiva. She is also worshipped at the lineage and community levels. Each family has its *mātā* (mother goddess) by which it maintains its identity with the lineage. Lineage *mātā* is worshipped during the *navarātra* festival in the month of *Kuār*. She is worshipped as per *tithi, sātam, aṭam, navamī* and the like. The people have been affected by the external invasions very often and migrated under compulsion. The bard maintains the links and keeps them informed about their ancestral village, the location of the temples of their lineage *bherū* and lineage *mātā*. They make the offerings facing in that direction so that it would reach their deity. *Mātā*-worship extends beyond caste-tribal limits.

As already said, there is a Śaktipīṭha at Ujjain which has a considerable influence in the countryside. Besides, there are a number of temples dedicated to goddess Kālikā or Kālkā. People of the rural areas are aware of goddess Hinglāj, the temple of which is said to be in Baluchistan (Pakistan). This desert goddess has great influence in rural Mālwā.

Lord Mahākāl is worshipped in *Dakṣinā mūrti* form. He faces south and not east — as normally seen — and the *jaladhārī*, too, channelises towards the east instead of north. The *tāntrikas* worship him in this form and this is a suggestion of a concrete link between this form of Lord Śiva and the spread of tāntrism in rural Mālwā. The Kālikā is the goddess mainly worshipped by *tāntrikas*. In rural Mālwā there are two *sampradāyas* that are related to Tāntric practices. The *tāntrika* sect has a good following from various tribal groups and castes.

Nāth samprādāya is popular in Mālwā. *Gṛhasthī nāth* and *Nāth-yogīs* are very common in Mālwā villages. Some *Nāths* act as priests, in the temples of the Scheduled Castes. *Nāth-yogīs* worship Lord Śiva as their principal deity. There is another group called *Māipanth*. Membership is restricted to the *panthīs* only. There are *māipanthīs* from tribal groups (Bhīls) as well as from other castes (like Banchda, a Scheduled Caste). It is almost a secret society and the rituals are performed in the *tāntrika* ways and very secretly. It is said that a light is kindled which is considered as divine light called *māijot* and it should not be seen by a non-member. If somebody sees it he has to join the *panth*. After the death of a kin, they perform a ritual which continues throughout the night and ends the next morning. It involves three phases — *māijot, bhairūjot* and *ujlājot*. It involves *tāntrika* practices and a goat offering is a must. Participants sing devotional songs throughout the night. From the type of songs other people come to know about the death and avoid going near the house out of fear of earning the wrath of the goddess. In this performance, the mother goddess is worshipped and offerings are also made to Lord Bhairū. The ritual ends with *ujlājot*.

Śiva-Pārvatī, the divine couple, are also worshipped in some festivals which are popular in rural Mālwā. *Gangor* is one such festival in which Umā-Maheśa is worshipped. Śiva-worship for the well-being of the husband and his long life is quite popular among the women-folk. They observe various festivals like *Vaṭ sāvitrī*. Śiva-worship in Mālwā is age-old and the tradition continues even today.

8

Résume

At this stage it is necessary to look back at the task we set for ourselves in this venture. We have to reconsider the objectives of the present work. Culture area may mean a largely homogeneous sub-region of a nation state. It need not be static and overlappings cannot be ruled out. Mālwā is a cultural area in this sense. Ujjain is the most important pilgrim centre of the area. We have attempted through the study of Ujjain and the Mahākāl temple, and the pattern of rituals and festivals to examine the commonness among various groups. The centre itself and its impact has been given utmost importance.

We have attempted to study, apart from the ritual behaviour taking Mahākāl as the nodule, the link that exists between the area and the centre and between centres. As Mahākāl is one of the incarnations of Lord Śiva, our observations mainly revolved around Lord Śiva and Śiva-worship.

We have seen that change of dynasties did not bring overall changes in the ritual observances or in the functioning of the pilgrim centre in the early Hindu period. The Muslim period has been marked as the period of destruction of temples and other buildings. The tradition remained alive to be revived during the Marāṭhā period. From this period to the contemporary period there has been a great interest in temple construction and detailed ritual observances. This has been discussed in the brief historical account.

Ujjain, the pilgrim centre, has a heterogeneous character. It shelters various temples, sects and traditions. It is a sacred place, and not merely owing to the presence of the Mahākāl temple. Many other factors have contributed to its sacred honour. The river Śiprā, the various *ghāṭs*, the crematoria, the pilgrims and the citizens — all have their own links with this holy city. The godmen have consolidated a countrywide network between the various sacred centres of India.

Ujjain is also known as Śrīkṣetra or Mahākāl *kṣetra*. A *tīrtha kṣetra* facilitates an empirical understanding of the universe for the common man. It is also represented in anthropomorphic form, which may lead to complete attainment of *mukti*. The holy circuit of Pañcakośī Ujjain, the *liṅga*-shaped Ujjain and the Mahākāl *svarūpa* in Ujjain make a perfect illustration of the symbolic structure. It is the microcosm and the geometrical meanings' transformation into symbolic structure that help in visual representation of a world-view. It also affirms the cosmic unity in the diversity of human cultures.

A *kṣetra* can only be understood within India's traditional vision of the world. Language and world-view are closely interlinked. The English word for *kṣetra* is the 'region' defined as a cohesive and homogeneous area marked by some common linguistic or cultural features. This is diametrically opposed to the Indian traditional osmocentric perception of *kṣetra* as a homology of the universe.

This holy *kṣetra* is the home for pious souls like saints and *gurus*. At the core of this *kṣetra* is Lord Mahākāleśvara. He is *anādi* — that is, having no beginning — and *ananta*, or having no end. It is *sāsvat* or ever-existing.

Mahākāleśvar is the tutelary deity of this *kṣetra* and the

Mahakal complex has a cluster of many temples. Rituals performed are related to *Paurāṇika*, Vedic and local traditions. There are professionals who live on the earnings of this temple. This main temple has several subsidiary temples that are linked with Lord Mahākāl. And finally there is a group of small Śiva temples spread all over the *kṣetra*. During the Muslim attacks, the Mahākāl temple was destroyed and other temples were also damaged. For the entire Muslim period, the main temple of Mahākāl was probably not there. This was reconstructed during Marāṭhā rule. In the Mahākāl temple the professionals have their rights well-defined and these have been inherited by them. The visitors are of three categories—local, regional and supraregional. It has a country-wide popularity and is one of the twelve prime self-effulgent *liṅga*s of India. In particular, it has relations with Oṁkāreśvar, the other *jyotirliṅga* of Mālwā. The temple of Mahākāleśvar has put Ujjain on the sacred map of India. Devotees include various castes and ethnic groups.

Ujjain has a two-fold role to play: firstly it is a pilgrim centre of India and secondly, it is the pilgrim centre of Mālwā. It is one of the four sites on earth for the *kumbha melā*. The *kumbha melā* is locally known as the *Siṁhastha melā*. At this great fair, ascetics and pilgrims gather in large numbers. They exchange views and organise religious discourses. Where the *akhāḍā*s or the saint organisations are concerned some organisational arrangements are made during this period. The *melā* involves hectic preparations in which the local administration, *akhāḍā*s, professionals, temples and finally the traders are busy. It is a great source of income for the professionals and traders. People of rural Mālwā also participate. Besides this *melā* there are other *yātrā*s and fairs which are attended mainly by the rural Mālvīs. The urbanites have less enthusiasm as far as the participation is concerned when compared to the rural people. The ritual pattern in the villages of Mālwā do not differ much among themselves and also from those of Ujjain. The villagers are not only aware of Ujjain and Mahākāl, but whenever they visit the city, they make it a point to have *darśana* of Lord Mahākāl. In *yātrās* they participate forming village-based groups. They visit Ujjain for performing the last rites for the deceased. The Brāhmaṇas and professionals like *kathāvācak*, etc., and the saints play a large role in keeping the tradition alive and maintaining the link. The saints live in some temples in the rural areas and visit their *akhāḍās* at Ujjain at intervals. Actually they maintain ties between Ujjain and other pilgrim centres, and between Ujjain and rural Mālwā.

Māch is the popular folk drama of Mālwā and Ujjain is the main centre from where the *Māch* troupes operate. And many *Māch* dramas are based on the socio-cultural background of Ujjain and the rural areas. Lord Bherū and *Mātā* (the mother goddess) worship are most popular in rural Mālwā.

Ujjain was one of the important trade centres of ancient India. Till the rapid growth of Indore in the recent past and its development into an industrialised city, Ujjain was the main commercial centre of Mālwā. It is still the centre as far as some specific trades are concerned. The trades related to worship of gods and goddesses have a special place at Ujjain and outside. Materials of use for making offerings are produced at the commercial level. They have a good market too. But the main trade is the selling of *pūṇya* and ridding one of one's sins. Ujjain provides a good earning for the brāhmaṇa group. They are specialised in various jobs, like *kathāvācana, pravacana, pāṭha, jāpa, tapa* in temples and simply putting a *tilak* or blessings fetch them money. Besides, they can accept *dāna.* There are *tīrtha purohits* to perform specific rituals for the visiting pilgrims. For a better living they always try to impress upon the pilgrims the greatness of Ujjain. Temples are also the source of livelihood for the brāhmaṇas. They maintain the atmosphere of mysticism all over. There are strategies to earn more from the visitors and these are passed on from generation to generation. A boy at an early stage becomes conscious of his priestly status and role. He also shows the *avaymudrā* to pilgrims sometimes twice his age. Like in other pilgrim centres of India, the *tīrtha purohits* here have *jajmānī* relations with pilgrims from distant places over the generations and they maintain detailed records. A *tīrtha purohit* does not offer his services to the *jajmān* of the other. They also have trade symbols like *nāhārvālā, dābbāvāla, hātivālā,* etc.

Śiva-worship in Mālwā is age-old. There are temples of Śiva belonging to three categories. In one group, the temples are small and sometimes only the *liṅga* is installed on a raised platform. Each village has a place of Śiva-worship in Mālwā. A category includes Śiva temples that are popular in the neighbourhood and the temples in this case are fairly elaborate. A fair is organised on the eve of some festival. The fairs are arranged in such a way that the festivals do not clash. They find a mention in the *Purāṇas* or great epics and in various other writings. And there are two *jyotirliṅgas*, Oṁkāreśvar and Mahākāleśvar whose popularity has crossed the limits of Mālwā. These may be considered under the third category. The association of the *kūmbha melā*, Śaktipītha and Vaiṣṇavite temples with Ujjain have made it the supreme pilgrim centre of Mālwā.

Bherū or Bhairava is considered as part of Lord Śiva and created by him and *mātā* is the form of Pārvatī, the consort of Lord Śiva. There are important Bhairava temples at Ujjain and a number of *devī* temples. Bherū and *mātā*-worship are very popular in rural Mālwā and they are worshipped at individual, lineage and community levels. The staple diet of Mālwā is offered as *naivedya* to these deities. Bherū is present in every sphere of their life. He is their protector who is responsible for good harvests and for their success in staging their folk dramas among other things. Bherū is the god of *Māch*, the folk drama.

Lord Mahākāl's form is the form of Lord Śiva, worshipped by the *tāntrikas*. He is *dakṣiṇāmūrti* (south-facing) here. There are two *sampradāyas* who profess tāntrism in rural Mālwā. They have followers from various castes as well as tribal groups. Again, Bhairū and *Māta*-worship is common among the caste and tribal groups. Some of the tribal groups believe that they have been created and protected by Lord Śiva. A dog, they believe, is their protector and a dog is the companion of Lord Bhairava. Dogs are not ill-treated as it may invite the wrath of Lord Bhairava.

From the foregoing chapters, a few aspects are clear. Firstly Mālwā is a geo-cultural and historical unit. It has a geographical demarcation and throughout the historical period it has remained one unit with occasional changes in the territorial boundaries. As Avantī it was one of the sixteen *janapadas* of ancient India. Avantī became Mālwā after the ruler's ethnic identity but remained more or less the same unit. The changes in the territories were fewer during Muslim rule. Under the Marāṭhā confedaracy, it was divided among four Marāṭhā *sardārs*. Finally, the whole area was annexed to the Indian union and at present it is a part of the largest state of the country. Avantikā or the present-day Ujjain remained the centre of political power for several centuries with minor break-ups.

In this culture area of Mālwā, Ujjain is the main centre of pilgrimage. It is heterogeneous in character as it houses temples of various sects of regional and national importance. Again it is the place of Lord Mahākāleśvar. Lord Mahākāl is the tutelary deity of Ujjain and hence the most important one. Ujjain maintains links with the sub-regions of Mālwā and has contacts with the rural folk at the lowest level. Actually it holds a pivotal position; and its link with the pilgrim centres of regional and supra-regional importance is mainly maintained by the organisations of various godmen, sects and *akhāḍās*.

There are professionals in priestly activities and Ujjain provides them a good pasture. It is a centre where Brāhmaṇas come for a living in their 'traditional trade'. The sacred performances have been commercialised to a considerable extent.

The priests actually 'sell' *puṇya* to the devotees. An enduring relationship is maintained between the *tīrtha purohit* and *jajmān*. Temples are often constructed not only out of *bhakti* but to earn money. The religious services like *jāpa, pāṭha*, etc. are available on payment. For a rich *jajmān* who wishes to spend more money, the performance will be more detailed. As a priest remarked, "One has to put in labour to earn."

Śiva-worship is common in rural and urban Mālwā and, of course, at Ujjain. This has cut across the 'tribe-caste' boundary. Lord Śiva and Bhairū have been closely related; in fact, it has been 'parochialised'. *Mātā* is a part of Pārvatī, the consort of Lord Śiva. Śiva-worship has a pattern by itself in Mālwā in the form of Bherū and Mahākāl has relations with the *tāntrika* sect. Bherū and *mātā* protect the people in the village. There are some festivals in which Umā-Maheśa is worshipped. Bherū-worship and *Mātā*-worship involve the castes as well as the tribes.

Visuals

Description of Visuals

Pl. 1. The temple of Lord Mahākāl, the ruling deity of Ujjain.

Pl. 2. The holy *liṅga* of Lord Mahākāl, one of the 12 *jyotirliṅgas* (self-effulgent) of India. It is *swayambhū* (not 'installed').

Pl. 3. The popular *bhāt-pūjan* of Lord Mahākāl in which the *liṅga* and the *jaladhārī* are covered with a thick coat of rice mixed with milk and ghee and *laghurudrābhiṣeka* is performed.

Pl. 4. The *ghṛt-pūjan*: A large number of devotees come to see Lord Mahākāl ornamented with frozen *ghī* slices and attend the *laghurudrābhiṣeka*.

Pl. 5. The sacred *Koṭitīrtha kuṇḍa* of Mahākāl temple which is said to contain the water of one crore *tīrthas*.

Pl. 6. The rear *sabhāmaṇḍapa* where the *paṇḍās*, the serving priests, sit. Hereditary rules are observed for the right of sitting on the seats (*takhtas*).

Pl. 7. The conch-shell gate of Mahākāl temple which was removed before the 1980 *siṁhastha* (*kumbha*) *mela* as part of renovation work by the authorities.

Pl. 8. The Rudra Sāgar is the largest of the seven sacred lakes of Ujjain which have now either become dry or are too shallow to hold water. In the backdrop is the Mahākāleśvara temple.

Pl. 9. The Bridhkāleśvara temple, believed to be older than the

Mahākāl temple. In the absence of the Mahākāl temple, devotees made offerings at this temple.

Pl. 10. Mātā Harsiddhi Devī temple, the most venerated *devi* temple in Ujjain.

Pl. 11. Gaḍh Kālikā or temple of Kālikā, the propitiating goddess of *kavi* Kālidāsa.

Pl. 12. The Kāliādah Palace, a summer palace, was originally a sun temple. Here is an image of Lord Sūrya.

Pl. 13. The *ghāṭs* of the holy river Śiprā — place for *siṁhastha snān.* Ujjain is one of the four sacred sites for the *kumbha mela* held every 12 years.

Pl. 1. The temple of Lord Mahākāl.

Pl. 2. The holy *liṅga* of Lord Mahākāl.

Pl. 4. The *ghṛt-pūjan*.

Pl. 5. The sacred *Koṭitīrtha kuṇḍa* of Mahākāl temple.

Pl. 6. The rear *sabhāmaṇḍapa* where the *paṇḍās* sit.

Pl. 7. The conch-shell gate of Mahākāl temple.

Pl. 8. The Rudra Sāgar, one of the sacred lakes of Ujjain. In the backdrop is the Mahākāleśvara temple.

Pl. 9. The Bridhkāleśvara temple.

Pl. 10. Mātā Harsiddhi Devī temple.

Pl. 11. Gaḍh Kālikā or temple of Kālikā.

Pl. 12. The Kāliādah Palace.

Pl. 13. The *ghāṭ*s of the holy river Śiprā — place for *siṁhastha snān*.

Glossary

Āvāhana	:	Invocation.
Ābhūṣaṇakakṣa	:	Room for keeping ornaments.
Abhiṣeka	:	Sacred investiture.
Abhiṣekapātra	:	Pot used for dropping water over the sacred *liṅga*.
Ācārya	:	A preceptor.
Adhikmās	:	Additional month as per Indian Astrology.
Ādigauḍa	:	Traditional brāhmaṇa group of Āryāvarta.
Ādināth	:	A saint of *Nāth* sect.
Ādi Śaṅkara	:	First Śaṅkarācārya.
Āditya	:	The son of Aditi.
Agarbattī	:	Camphor sticks.
Agasteśvar Mahādeva	:	Lord Mahādeva who blessed saint Agastya.
Aghorī	:	Member of an order of mendicants who worship Śiva.
Agni	:	The god of fire.
Agnisnān	:	Fire bath.
Āgneya	:	Pertaining to fire.
Ājopāl	:	Deity who guards the village.
Akhaṇḍa	:	Indivisible.
Akhaṇḍa āśrama	:	Follower of a *Śaiva* sect.
Akhaṇḍa dhūnī	:	Uninterrupted sacred fire.

Akṣaya vaṭa	:	Undecaying sacred banian tree.
Alakhadhām	:	Centre of the mendicants of *Alakha* sect.
Ālvar sant	:	A saint from Ālwar (Rajasthan)
Amṛta	:	Nectar ambrosia.
Amṛta mātra-naivedyam	:	A small amount of sweet offered with nector.
Anādi	:	Eternal offering.
Anādi kalpeś-vara Mahādeva	:	Lord Mahādeva ever existing.
Ānanda	:	Tranquillity.
Ananta	:	Immortal
Annadāna	:	Donating cereals as gift.
Annapūrṇā devī	:	Goddess of wealth.
Antimasnān	:	Final bath.
Ānūnā	:	Without salt.
Araṇya	:	Forest (one of Daśanāmī group) of saints.
Ardhakumbha	:	*Kumbha* congregation held between two *pūrṇa kumbhas* (that is, after 6 years).
Arundhatī	:	Revered lady saint of Saptarṣi (seven saints).
Āryāvarta	:	Area of Vindhya hills.
Āṣāḍha	:	Indian month (June-July).
Āsanas	:	*Yogik* postures.
Āśrama	:	Hermitage.
Aśubha karma	:	Inauspicious rites.
Aśubha śrāddha	:	Inauspicious mortuary rites.
Aṣṭādhyāyī	:	Pāṇini's famous treatise of grammar.
Aṣṭakoṇa	:	Octagonal.

Aṣṭatīrtha	:	Visiting eight sacred places.
Asura	:	A demon.
Aśvakrāntā	:	*Śākta* way of ḍividing the Āryāvarta.
Āśvalāyana Śrauta Sūtra	:	One of the *Sūtras* or sacred texts.
Aśvamedha yajña	:	Horse sacrifice.
Aṭal	:	Unmoved.
Āṭam	:	Eighth day of fortnight (dark or bright half).
Avantī	:	Old name of Ujjain; a republic of ancient India.
Avantikā	:	A republic of ancient India.
Avantya apabhraṃśa	:	Dialect of Avantī.
Baḍā	:	Big/large.
Baḍā Gaṇeśa	:	Gaṇeśa idol of enormous size.
Baidyanātha	:	One of twelve sacred *jyotirliṅgas*.
Bairāgī	:	*Vaiṣṇava* mendicant.
Baiṭhak	:	Centres of Vallabha *sampradāya.*
Bāṇagaṅgā	:	Stream believed to have been produced by Lakṣmaṇa by striking an arrow.
Baṃśīvaṭa	:	The big tree under which Kṛṣṇa played on his flute.
Baudhāyana	:	Author of *Dharmasūtra* who lived between 1400 and 800 BC.
Bhādon	:	Indian month (August-September)
Bhagavān	:	The supreme being.
Bhairava	:	Lord Śiva or his forms.
Bhairavāṣṭamī	:	Auspicious day for Bhairava-worship.

Bhairūjot : Sacred light of Lord Bhairava.

Bhairū pūṇam : Full moon day when Bhairava is worshipped.

Bhakta Prahalāda : Prahlāda the pious.

Bhaṇḍārā : A feast given to mendicants.

Bhāṅg kā śṛṅgār : Adornment with *bhāṅg* paste.

Bhāraṭī : A section of Ḍaśanāmī saints.

Bhartṛhari : King of Ujjain who became *Nāth* saint.

Bhasmasnān : Smearing the *liṅga* with ashes.

Bhasmāratī : Offering ash.

Bhātpūjan : Offering boiled rice.

Bhīmaśaṅkara : One of the twelve *jyotirliṅgas*.

Bhog : Food offered to an idol.

Bhogliṅga : Tutelary deity of Śṛṅgerī Śaṅkarācārya *maṭha*.

Bhojana : Meal.

Bhūrīmātā : Yellow soil.

Bhuśuṇḍī Kāk : Divine crow.

Bhuteśvara Mahādevā : Lord Śiva.

Bijlī : Electricity

Bikāl Bhairava : A Bhairava.

Bilva patra : Leaves of Aegle Marmelos, the wood-apple tree (*Bel*).

Bīrliṅga : Tutelary diety of Nepal.

Bor : Plum.

Baudhavaṭ : Holy fig tree under which Gautama Buddha gained enlightenment.

Brahmā : One of the three triads of Hindu

		mythology.
Brāhmaṇa	:	The theological portion of the *Veda*s.
Brahma Satra	:	Organising lectures on supreme spirit.
Bṛhadāraṇyaka	:	One of the *Upaniṣads*.
Bṛhaspateśvar Mahādeva	:	Lord Śiva.
Bṛhaspati	:	The preceptor of gods.
Caḍhotrī	:	Offering of a God.
Cait	:	Pertaining to the month of *caitra* (March-April).
Caitra	:	First month (March-April) of Hindu year.
Caitra budhavārs	:	Wednesdays of the month of *Caitra*.
Cait-se-jeṭh	:	From month *Caitra* (March-April) to month *Jyeṣṭha* (May-June).
Cakratīrtha	:	A cremation ground.
Cālīs Liṅgeśvar	:	Lord Śiva.
Camatkār	:	Amazement.
Camelī	:	Jasmine flower.
Campā	:	Michelia Champacca.
Cāmuṇḍā mātā	:	Goddess Cāmuṇḍā.
Candan Lobān	:	Frankincense.
Cāndnī	:	Moonlight.
Carmanvatī	:	River Cambal.
Cāra dhāma	:	Four very sacred centres of Hindus.
Carkhā	:	Spinning wheel.
Caśmā	:	Sections.
Caturdaśī śrāddha	:	Final mortuary rites performed on 14th day after death.
Caubīs khambā	:	Structure of twenty-four pillars.

Caurāsī	:	Eighty-four.
Caurāsī liṅga	:	Eighty-four *liṅgas*.
Cauth	:	Tax.
Chappan pakavān	:	Detail food offering.
Chatrī	:	Cenotaph.
Chatrī Cowk	:	Square near the cenotaph of late Gwalior King.
Chenāti	:	Cluster of six brāhmaṇa groups.
Choṭā	:	Younger.
Cintāharaṇa	:	That which takes away all worries.
Cintāman Gaṇapati	:	Lord Gaṇeśa.
Ḍabbāvālā	:	One who has *dabbā* (box) for a trademark.
Dadupaṅthī	:	A religious sect.
Dahī	:	Curd.
Dakṣiṇā	:	Present given to a priest.
Dakṣiṇī	:	Southern.
Dakṣināmūrti	:	Facing south.
Dālān	:	Antechamber.
Dālbāṭī	:	Pulse and baked bread.
Ḍamru	:	Small drum.
Dāna	:	Gift.
Dānagrahīta	:	Person who accepts gift.
Dānapeṭī	:	Box for putting the gifts.
Darśana	:	Divine visitation.
Daśamī	:	Tenth day of bright or dark half of a month.
Daśanāmī gṛhasthīs	:	Householders of *Daśanāmī* order.

Daśaharā	:	A Hindu festival.
Daśavā	:	Final mortuary rite.
Dātā	:	Gift-giver.
Dattā ākhāḍā	:	An organisation of saints.
Dābhe	:	Division in *akhāḍās*.
Devālaya	:	House of God/Temple.
Dīpak	:	Lamp.
Dīpamālikā	:	Stand for row of lighted lamps.
Devī	:	Mother Goddess.
Devī Annapūrṇā	:	Goddess Aṇṇapūrṇā.
Devī Darśana	:	Divine visitation of Mother Goddess.
Devī pūjan	:	Worshipping the Mother Goddess.
Devī yantra	:	Geometric figure for *devī*-worship.
Deva uṭhni egāras	:	Eleventh day of *Kārtik* month.
Dīvān	:	A court minister.
Dīvālī	:	Festival of light.
Dhāmas	:	Sacred centre.
Dharmaśālā	:	A rest house for pilgrims.
Dharmanāth	:	Saint of *Nāth* sect.
Dharmasūtra	:	Name of a Jaina treatise.
Dhatūrā	:	The thorn apple.
Dhyān	:	Meditation.
Ḍholī	:	Drummer.
Dhotī	:	Loin cloth.
Dhruva	:	Motionless.
Dhulaṇḍī	:	Festival of colour.
Dhūpāratī	:	To incense.
Dīā	:	Lamp.

Digambar	:	Sky clad; a class of ascetics.
Ḍol	:	Palanquin.
Ḍol egāras	:	Festival observed by *Vaiṣṇavas*.
Dūdh	:	Milk.
Dvādaśa	:	Twelve.
Dvāpar	:	The third of the four ages.
Dvārkādhīśa	:	Tutelary god of Dvārkā.
Dvārapāla	:	Gatekeeper deity.
Dvaitavāda	:	Duality in religious philosophy.
Dvaitādvaitavāda	:	Philosophy of monotheism and dualism.
Ebrāmātā	:	Goddess Ebrā.
Ekādaśa Liṅgeśvar	:	Lord Śiva.
Ekādaśa mahimnāstotra, *Ekmahimnā stotra*	:	Famous hymn of praise for Lord Śiva.
Gaddī	:	Seat/Centre.
Gaḍkālikā	:	Goddess Kālikā of the Forte.
Gaṇa	:	An attendant.
Gaṇapati	:	Lord Gaṇeśa.
Gandha	:	Fragrance.
Gaṅgānāth	:	Saint of *Nāth* order.
Garbhagṛha	:	Sanctum-sanctorum.
Garjāri Apabhraṃśa	:	Dialect.
Ger	:	Religious procession.
Ghaḍyāl	:	Alligator.
Ghāṭ	:	Bathing place on river bank.
Ghineśvara	:	Lor l Śiva.

Ghṛt-pūjan	:	Special offering of clarified butter.
Giri	:	*Daśanāmī* saints.
Gangor	:	Folk festival.
Gopāl	:	Lord Viṣṇu.
Gopuram	:	Decorated gateway of a temple.
Gorā	:	Fair complexioned.
Gorā Bhirava	:	Bhairava.
Gorakhnāth	:	Saint of *Nāth* order.
Gosāin	:	Saint of *Daśanāmī* order.
Gotra Bhairava	:	Bhairava for *gotra* members.
Govindeśvara Mahādeva	:	Lord Śiva.
Gṛhasthī	:	Householder.
Grām bherū	:	Bhairava protecting the village.
Guḍi Paḍbā	:	New year day.
Gulāb	:	Rose.
Gulāl	:	Red farinaceous powder.
Haihaiya	:	A royal dynasty.
Hanumān Jayantī	:	Birthday celebration of Lord Hanumān.
Hariharabhenṭ	:	Meeting of Lord Hari and Lord Hara.
Harsiddhimātā	:	Goddess Harisiddhi.
Haritālikā	:	A festival.
Haṭakeśaram	:	One of the twelve *jyotirliṅgas*.
Hātivālā	:	A trademark of *tīrtha purohits*.
Haṭa-yogī	:	An ascetic who performs austerity.
Hiṃlāj	:	Goddess Hiṅglāj.
Hiraṇya Kaśyapa	:	Demon King.

Holī	:	Festival.
Indreśvar	:	Lord Mahādeva.
Īṣṭadevī	:	Tutelary goddess.
Itra	:	Perfume.
Jajmān	:	Patron.
Jaladhārī	:	The cup in which the phallus is fixed.
Jalasnān	:	Water bath.
Janapada	:	Ancient Republic.
Janmāṣṭamī	:	Birthday of Lord Kṛṣṇa.
Jāpa	:	Muttering of prayers/adoration.
Jayater Bhriśa vāhana	:	Long live the bull flag.
Jhaṇḍā	:	Flag.
Jhāṅkī	:	Tableau.
Jhāñja	:	Cymbals.
Jyotirliṅga	:	Self-effulgent *liṅga.*
Jyotirliṅga Mahākāl	:	An epithet of Śiva.
Jyotirmaṭh	:	Northern Maṭh of Śaṅkarācārya.
Jeri	:	Silver embroidery work.
Junā	:	Old.
Junā Mahākāl	:	Old Mahākāl.
Juthikā	:	Jasmine.
Kabīrpanthī	:	A religious sect.
Kaccā dhāgā	:	Raw thread.
Kahār	:	Community of palanquin bearers.
Kailāsa	:	An epithet of Śiva.
Kālā	:	Dark.
Kalaśa	:	Ornamentation on temple dome.
Kālabhairava	:	Chief attendant of Lord Śiva.

Kāliādeh	:	Summer palace.
Kāliāpīr	:	Burial of a Muslim saint.
Kālidāsa	:	Legendary poet.
Kālīmaṭṭī	:	Black soil.
Kaliyuga	:	The fourth of the four ages.
Kālikā	:	Goddess Kālī.
Kālon-kā-kāl	:	Lord of death.
Kalpavṛkṣa	:	Divine tree which yields anything desired.
Kāmkoṭipīṭha	:	Śaṅkara Maṭh of Śṛṅgerī.
Kaṇḍā	:	Dried cow dung cake.
Kanphaṭa Yogī	:	*Nāth* saints.
Kāpālika	:	An epithet of Lord Śiva.
Kapilnāth	:	A *Nāth* saint.
Karkoṭaka Nāga	:	Ancient tribal community.
Karpūrārtī	:	To camphor.
Kārtik pūnam	:	Full moon day of the month of *Kārtik*.
Kārtik snān	:	Holy bath on the full moon day of *Kārtik*.
Kārtik Svāmī	:	Lord Kārtik.
Kāśī Viśvanāth	:	Lord Viśvanāth of Kāśī.
Kāśyapa	:	Saint Kāśyapa.
Kastūrī	:	Musk.
Kathā	:	A religious discourse.
Kathāvācak	:	Person who gives religious discourses.
Kātya	:	Brāhmaṇa who performs last rites.
Kedārnāth	:	An epithet of Śiva.
Khākī	:	A saint organisation.
Khalāsī	:	One who keeps the temple clean.
Khāṇḍaveśvar	:	Lord Khāṇḍaveśvar.
Khaṭṭā	:	Sour.

Khayāl	:	Folk drama of Mewar.
Kheḍā bherū	:	Bhairava of the farm land.
Khīr	:	Sweet dish.
Khīrsāgar	:	A lake.
Kumbha snān	:	Holy bath during *Kumbha* congregation.
Kṣetra	:	A place of pilgrimage.
Kuār	:	Indian month (October-November).
Kuār daśahara	:	Dussehra festival of *Kuār* month.
Kula bherū	:	Bhairava of lineage members.
Kumbha melā	:	*Kumbha* congregation.
Kumkum	:	Saffron.
Kuṇḍa	:	Sacred pond.
Kuṇḍal	:	Ear-ring.
Lakṣmī	:	Goddess of wealth.
Lakṣmīnāth	:	Lord of Goddess Lakṣmī.
Lālbāī-Phūlbāī	:	Goddess of pox and measles.
Lord Kūrma	:	Tortoise god.
Lord Narasiṁha	:	An incarnation of Lord Viṣṇu.
Lord Māruti	:	Monkey god.
Lord Sūrya	:	Sun god.
Māch	:	Folk theatre of Mālwā.
Machindranāth	:	Saint of *Nāth* order.
Mādhava	:	An epithet of Lord Viṣṇu.
Mādis	:	Decision in saint organisation.
Madhyāhna-kālīna	:	Noon time.
Mahābhog	:	Great offering.
Magar	:	Alligator.
Mahallā	:	Ward/Hamlet.

Mahājanapada	Great ancient republic.
Mahant	Head of a *Maṭh.*
Mahānirvāṇī	Final Beatitude
Mahāsabhā	Great congregation.
Mahānirvāṇī akhāḍā	A saint organisation.
Māījot	Sacred light of mother goddess.
Māīpantha	Follower of *Śākta* order.
Maithuna	Sex act.
Mallikārjuna	A god.
Mālpoā	A sweet.
Mālwā	Tableland of central India.
Māmleśvara	An epithet of Lord Śiva.
Māṇḍnā	Floor painting.
Maṅgalnāth	An epithet of Śiva.
Maṇikarnikā ghāṭ	Sacred cremation ground of Kāśī.
Mañjaris	Triangular structures of the temple dome.
Mankeśvar	Lord Śiva.
Māṃsa	Meat.
Mantra puṣpāñjali	Offering incantation and flower.
Mārgaśīrṣa	A month in Hindu calendar (November-December).
Maśālcī	Torch-bearer.
Mātā	Mother goddess.
Maṭha	Centre of saint organisation.
Maṭhāmnaya	Code of conduct for saint organisation.
Mātṛkā	Mother goddess.
Mṛcchakaṭika	A famous play written by Śūdraka.
Mauḍeśvari	Tutelary goddess of Mauḍ brāhmaṇas.

Meghadūta	:	A famous play by legendary poet Kālidāsa.
Mīṭhā	:	Sweet.
Mogrā	:	A kind of jasmine.
Mokṣaliṅga	:	An epithet of Lord Śiva.
Mṛtyuloka	:	Mortal world.
Mukti	:	Salvation.
Muktiliṅga	:	Sacred *liṅga* which gives salvation.
Navamī	:	Ninth day of each fortnight of lunar month.
Nagāḍākhānā	:	Place where large kettledrums are kept.
Nagāḍā	:	Large kettledrum.
Nagārcī	:	Kettledrum player.
Nagar pradakṣiṇā	:	Taking round of a city.
Nāgbali	:	Funeral rites.
Nāgcandreśvar	:	An epithet of Lord Śiva.
Nāgeśvar	:	An epithet of Śiva.
Nāgnāth	:	Saint of *Nāth* order.
Nāg pañcamī	:	Festival in which snake god is worshipped.
Nāhārvālā	:	Trademark of a *paṇḍā* family.
Naimittika	:	Casual.
Naivedya	:	Oblation.
Namak camak	:	A kind of offering.
Nāmdevpanth	:	A *Vaiṣṇava* sect.
Namkīn	:	Salty.
Nandī	:	Sacred bull of Śiva.
Nārāyaṇa bali	:	Funeral rites.
Nārāyaṇa Dev	:	A *Vaiṣṇava* saint.

Narasiṁha ghāṭ	:	*Ghāṭ* on Śiprā bank.
Nāth	:	A sect of *Śaiva* order.
Nāth-yogī	:	Saint of *Nāth* sect.
Navagraha	:	Nine planet god.
Navagraha mandir	:	Temple of nine planets.
Navarātra	:	First nine days of the bright half of *Āśvin* or *Caitra*.
Nāvi	:	Navel.
Navraṅga	:	Of new design.
Nāyab Tehasildār	:	A revenue official.
Nīlakaṇṭheśvar Mahādeva	:	An epithet of Lord Śiva.
Nimbārka	:	Nambāditya.
Nirālambī	:	One without a support.
Nirañjanī	:	A saint organisation.
Nirīkṣaka	:	An inspector.
Nirmohī	:	An organisation of saints.
Nirvāṇī	:	An organisation of saints.
Nitya	:	Regular.
Nivārī	:	Used in Śiva-worship.
Nyās	:	Pledge.
Oṁkāreśvar Mahādeva	:	An epithet of Śiva.
Pabnāth	:	*Nāth* saint.
Pāgalnāth	:	*Nāth* saint.
Pānca	:	Five.
Pañcāmṛta	:	A mixture consisting of milk, curd, sugar, honey and clarified butter offered to a deity.

Pañca-mukhoṭā-kā-darśana	:	Having *darśana* of the five-masked.
Pañcaraṅgī	:	Five-coloured.
Pañca devatā	:	Five main gods of worship, namely, Sun, Śiva, Viṣṇu, Gaṇeśa and Devī.
Pañca Draviḍa	:	Five brāhmaṇa groups — Mahārāṣṭra, Telaṅga, Karnāṭ, Gujarāt and Draviḍa.
Pañca Gauḍ	:	Five brāhmaṇa groups — Sarasvatī, Kānyakubja, Gaura, Maithilī and Utkal.
Pāncakośī	:	Pilgrimage round the city of Ujjain.
Pañca-Mukhī Hanumān	:	Lord Hanumān having five faces.
Paṇḍā	:	Serving priests of sacred centres.
Pāṇini	:	A Sanskrit scholar.
Pārad	:	Quick silver.
Paraśurāma	:	Legendary brāhmaṇa saint.
Pārāyaṇa	:	Reading a book from beginning to end.
Parmār	:	Rājpūt clan.
Parvat	:	Hill.
Pārvatī	:	Consort of Lord Śiva.
Paśupatināth	:	An epithet of Śiva.
Pātāl Bhairava	:	Lord Bhairava of infernal regions.
Pātāleśvara	:	An epithet of Śiva.
Pāṭh	:	Reading.
Peḍā	:	A sweet.
Pīpal	:	Fig tree.
Phālgūn	:	Last month according to Indian year (February-March).
Piāo	:	Drinking water hut.
Pīrjī	:	Muslim saint.

Pisāca Mukteśvara Ghat	:	A bathing place on Śiprā bank.
Pīṭhas	:	Very sacred centres of Devi worship.
Pūnam	:	Full Moon.
Pravacana	:	An elucidation.
Pradoṣa	:	Sunset.
Praṇāmī	:	A sect.
Prāṇāyāms	:	The process of restraining breath.
Prasād	:	Food offered to an idol.
Prātaḥkālina	:	Early morning/day break.
Prātaḥkālīna pūjā	:	Morning offerings.
Pratihāras	:	A ruling dynasty.
Pratipadā	:	First day of each half of the lunar month.
Pūjan sāhitya/ pūjan sāmagrī	:	Items necessary for making offerings.
Pujārī	:	Priest.
Pujārinī	:	A woman who propitiates God by making offerings.
Punjābī	:	A language.
Puṇya	:	Piety.
Rādhā/Rādhikā	:	Divine consort of Lord Kṛṣṇa.
Rājā	:	King.
Rājmal ghāṭ	:	Bathing place on Śiprā bank.
Rākhī	:	The amulet which is tied to a person on the *Rakṣābandhan* festival.
Rāmānandī	:	A *Vaiṣṇava* sect.
Rāmānuja	:	A *Vaiṣṇava* saint.
Rāmcandra Bābā	:	A saint.
Rāmeśvar	:	An epithet of Lord Śiva.

Rāmghāṭ	:	Bathing place on Śiprā bank where Lord Rāma performed last rites.
Rāṇ Mukteśvar	:	An epithet on Lord Śiva.
Rāmnavamī	:	Birthday of Lord Rāma.
Raṅgīn nāḍā	:	Coloured cotton loops.
Rāsyātrā	:	Festival in memory of the dances of Lord Kṛṣṇa and the cowherds.
Rathakrānta	:	Śākta way of dividing the Anpalrarta.
Ratnākar Sāgar	:	One of the seven ancient lakes of Ujjain.
Ravi Veda Dhām	:	School where Vedic traditions are taught.
Revatī	:	The twenty-seventh *nakṣatra*.
Ṛgvedī Padma-pād	:	Saint Padmapad.
Rogyādevī	:	A goddess of diseases.
Rudra	:	The eleven manifestations of Lord Śiva.
Rudrākṣa	:	The seeds of the tree *eleocorpus ganitrus*.
Rudrākṣamālā	:	A garland of *rudrākṣa*.
Rudra Sāgar	:	One of the seven sacred ancient lakes of Ujjain.
Rudrāṣṭakas	:	Couplets chanted while making offerings to Lord Rudra.
Rudra tantra	;	Sacred geometrical figure symbolising Lord Rudra.
Sabhāgṛha	:	Antechamber.
Sabhāmaṇḍapa	:	Antechamber.
Sādhanā	:	Accomplish.
Sāfāivālā	:	Sweeper.
Sāgar	:	One of the *Daśanāmī* group.
Sahāyak pujārī	:	Person assisting the chief priest.

Śāhī snān	:	Royal bath.
Sākṣī Gopāl	:	An epithet of Lord Viṣṇu.
Samādhi	:	Tomb.
Sāmānya pūjan	:	Ordinary offerings.
Samiti	:	Committee.
Sampradāya	:	Organisations of saints.
Samudra-manthan	:	Divine sea churning.
Saṅgameśvara Mahādeva	:	An epithet of Lord Śiva.
Sāñjhā	:	A festival observed by girls of marriage able age.
Saṅkaṭmocan Siddh Hanumān	:	Lord Hanumān.
Santoṣī	:	An epithet of Goddess Pārvatī.
Saptarṣi	:	A group of seven stars.
Sarāfā	:	Where people trade in gold and silver ornaments.
Sarasvatī	:	Goddess of learning.
Sarasvatī Deva	:	A saint.
Sarasvatī satra	:	Ancient congress of scholars.
Śarbat	:	Sweet drink.
Sātam	:	Seventh day of dark or bright half.
Satpuḍā	:	Hill range.
Satyanāth	:	A *Nāth* saint.
Savāris	:	Religious procession.
Seharā-kā-śṛṅgāra	:	Decoration with flower chains.
Sevantī	:	White rose.
Śakas	:	Rulers of Śaka Dynasty.

Śākta	:	Worshipper of mother goddess.
Śāktamat	:	Philosophy of the Mother cult.
Śakti	:	Power divine as symbolic representation of Mother goddess.
Śakti Pīṭha	:	Ancient fifty-two centres of *Devī*-worship.
Śālivāhana	:	King of middle India.
Śāligrām	:	Lord Viṣṇu's idol.
Śani	:	Saturn.
Śani amāvasyā	:	Full dark day falling on Saturday.
Śaṅkarācārya	:	Great saint who propagated *Advaita* philosophy.
Śaṅkaramaṭha	:	*Maṭhas* established by Ādi Śaṅkarācārya.
Sāṁkhya	:	One of six schools of Hindu philosophy.
Svayambhu	:	Self-effulgent.
Śayanārati	:	Last offerings of the day.
Śiṅgā	:	A trumpet.
Sāuraseni Prākṛt	:	Old Prākṛt dialect.
Śrīnāthjī	:	An epithet of Lord Kṛṣṇa.
Śrīsomnāth	:	Lord Somnāth.
Śuddhādvaitavāda	:	A Hindu religious philosophy.
Śukla	:	Priest.
Śubhakarma	:	Pious action.
Śubhaśrāddha	:	Pious rites.
Siddhas	:	Accomplished.
Siddha Gaṇeśa	:	Lord Gaṇeśa who gives accomplishment.
Sidhnāth	:	An epithet of Lord Śiva.
Sidhnāth ghāṭ	:	Bathing place on Śiprā bank near Sidhnāth temple.
Śikhar	:	Temple dome.

Silṁavaṭ	:	Community of stone curvers.
Siṁhastha	:	*Kumba melā* held at Ujjain after twelve years.
Śītalāmātā	:	Goddess Śītalā.
Śiṣya	:	Disciple.
Skanda Purāṇa	:	A Hindu mythological text.
Śmaśān	:	Cremation ground.
Ṣoḍaśopacāra	:	Sixteen ingredients of worship.
Śolā Sāgar	:	One of the seven ancient lakes of Ujjain.
Somtī	:	Dark night falling on Monday.
Somtī Amāvasyā Snān	:	Taking bath on Somtī day.
Śrī	:	A religious sect.
Śrīgauḍa	:	A brāhmaṇa caste.
Śṛṅgār	:	Adornment.
Surā	:	Spirituous liquor.
Sūryamukhī	:	Facing sun.
Sūryamukhī Hanumān	:	Lord Hanumān facing sun or east.
Svapnavā-savadattam	:	Ancient drama written by Bhāsa.
Svapneśvar Mahādeva	:	An epithet of Lord Śiva.
Svarga	:	Heaven.
Svastik	:	Fylfot.
Takhtas	:	Cots.
Tap	:	Penance.
Tārakāliṅgam	:	An epithet of Lord Śiva.
Tārakāsur	:	A demon.
Telaṅga	:	A community of brāhmanas.

Ṭikā : Mark on the forehead.

Tilak : Mark of the forehead.

Tīja : Third day of the dark or bright half.

Tillī laḍḍu : Sweet made out of sugar and sesame.

Til saṅkrānti : Festival observed commemorating the beginning of solstice.

Tīrtha : Place of pilgrimage.

Tīrthapiṇḍa śrāddha : Last rites performed at specific pilgrim centres.

Tīrtha purohit : Priests serving pilgrims at pilgrim centres.

Tithi : A summer day.

Toṅgās : Horse-pulled carts.

Trayambakeśvar : An epithet of Lord Śiva.

Tribiṣṭhapeśvar Mahādeva : An epithet of Lord Śiva.

Tripiṇḍa : Oblations.

Tripurī : Lord Śiva.

Triśūla : Trident.

Tulsīmālā : Garland of Holy Basilwood.

Turā : Folk Drama.

Turā kalaṅgī : Folk Drama.

Udāsī ghāṭ : Bathing place on Śiprā bank.

Udāsīn gṛhasthī : Householder of *Udāsīn* order.

Ujlā Jot : Flame symbolising purification.

Umā-Maheśa : Lord Śiva and his consort Umā.

Uṇḍārā tālāb : A lake.

Uttarvāhinī : Flowing north.

Vāhana : Animal conveyance of deities.

Vaikuṇṭh caudas : Festival observed on the fourteenth day of the bright half of Kārtik.

Vaiṣṇava	:	Devotees of Lord Viṣṇu.
Vallabha	:	*Vaiṣṇava* saint organisation.
Vārkāri	:	Follower of *Vārkāri* sect.
Vārkāri pantha	:	A sect.
Varuṇa snān	:	Bath of Lord Varuṇa, the god of water.
Vasiṣṭha	:	Revered saint.
Vaśukī	:	Divine serpent; the second of the eight prominent *nāgas*.
Vaṭ-pīpal	:	Sacred trees symbolising the trinity — Brahmā, Viṣṇu and Maheśa.
Vaṭ-Sāvitrī	:	Festival observed by married ladies for the well-being of their husbands.
Veda pāṭhaśālā	:	School where Vedic rhymes are taught.
Vedaśālā	:	Observatory.
Vidiśā	:	Capital of an ancient kingdom.
Vikramāditya	:	Legendary king of Ujjain.
Vikrānt Bhairava	:	One-fourth of Lord Bhairava.
Vināyaka	:	An epithet of Lord Gaṇeśa.
Virakta	:	Detachment from worldly life.
Viśiṣṭādvaitavāda	:	A religious Hindu philosophy.
Viṣṇu Krāntā	:	A region of Āryāvarta as per *Śākta* Philosophy.
Viṣṇu Purāṇa	:	A Hindu mythological text.
Viṭṭhal Rukmā	:	Propitiating deities of Paṇḍharpur in Mahārāṣṭra.
Vitihotras	:	One of ruling dynasty.
Viṭṭhal Paṇḍhārī-nāth Vivāha	:	Propitiating deities of Paṇḍharpur marriage.
Viśvakarmā	:	The divine architect.
Viśvanāth	:	An epithet of Lord Śiva.

Vṛddha Kāleśvar	:	Old Mahākāleśvar.
Yadu	:	Member of Yadu race.
Yajñopavīta	:	Sacred thread.
Yajñaśālā	:	Sacrificial place.
Yajurveda	:	Third of the four *Veda*s.
Yantra	:	Symbolic expression of deities.
Yātrā	:	Pilgrimage.
Yātrī	:	Pilgrim.
Yena tvām rakṣā mānāhi rākṣanumā caumācāl	:	I am offering this. 'O' God you protect me.
Yogī	:	Religious mendicant.
Yoginī	:	Female mendicant.
Yogaliṅgam	:	Phallus born out of meditation.

Bibliography

Ambedkar, B.R., 1948, *The Untouchables*, Bombay.

Aurobindo, Śrī, 1939, *Essays on the Gita* (two vols.), Arya Publishing House, Calcutta.

Baden Pawell, B.H., 1896, *The Indian Village Community*, London.

Bhandarkar, R.G., 1923, *Vaisnavism, Saivism and minor religious systems*, Karl J. Trubner, Strassburg.

Bhattacharya, J.N., 1896, *Hindu Castes and Sects*, Calcutta.

Banerjee, B., 1931, "Possible Origin of the Caste System in India", in *Indian Antiquary*.

Bose, N.K., 1951, "Caste in India", in *Man India*, Vol. 31, Nos. 3 & 4.

Beuquct, A.C., 1948, *Hinduism*, Hutchinson's University Library.

Briggs, G.N., *Gorakhnath and the Kanphata Yogis*, Calcutta.

Census of India, 1931, Vol. 20, Part I.

Carstairs, G.M., 1954, "Daru and Bhang, Cultural Factors in the choice of Intoxicant", in *Quarterly Journal of studies on Alcohol*, Vol. 15.

Clark Wisslar, 1965, *Man and Culture*, New York.

Coomaraswami, A.K., 1948, *The Dance of Shiva*, Bombay.

Crooke, W., 1926, *Religion and Folklore of Northern India*.

Danda, A.K., 1972, *Eastern Anthropologist*, Vol. 25, No. I.

Dowson, J.A., 1950, *A Classical Dictionary of Hindu Mythology*, London.

Dubios, Abbe, *Hindu manner, customs and ceremonies* (tr. by Henry K. Beauchamp), Oxford.

Durkheim, E., 1954, *Elementary Forms of Religious Life.*

Farquehra, J.N., 1913, *The Crown of Hinduism.*

Forde, D., 1934, *Habitat, Economy and Society.*

Fuchs, S., 1950, *The Children of Hari, A study of the Nimal Balahis in the C.P. of India*, Vienna.

Ghurye, G.S., 1951, *Caste and Class in India*, Bombay.

Hastings, J. (ed.), 1952, *Encyclopaedia of Religion and Ethics*, Vols. 2, 5, 6, 11 & 12, T & T. Clark, Edinburgh.

Kane, P.V., 1930, *History of Dharmasastras.*

Karve, I., 1961, *Hindu Society — An Interpretation*, Poona.

Law, B.C., *Ancient India.*

Macdonnel, A.A., 1927, *India's Past*, Oxford.

Majumdar, D.N., 1948, *Matrix of Indian Culture*, Lucknow.

———, 1958, *Races and Cultures of India*, Bombay.

Majumdar, R.C. and A.D. Pusalkar (Ed.), 1952, *The Vedic Age*, Bombay.

———, 1953, *The Age of Imperial Unity*, Bombay.

———, 1954, *The Classical Age*, Bombay.

Malinowski, B., 1944, *A Scientific Theory of Culture and other Essays.*

Malcolm, J., 1923, *Central India*, Vols. 1 & 2.

Marriot Mckim (Ed.), 1955, *Village India*, American Anthropological Association.

Mayer, A.C., 1955, "Change in a Malwa village", in *Economic Weekly*, Vol. 7, No. 39.

———, 1960, *Caste and Kinship — A Village and its Religion in Central India.*

Mathur, K.S., *Caste and Ritual in a Malwa Village.*

Menon, V.P., 1956, *The Story of Integration of States.*

Milton Singar and Morgan K.W. (ed.), 1953, *The Religion of the Hindus.*

Mukherjee, Radhakumud, 1956, *Ancient India*, Indian Press, Allahabad.

Nobel Margaret Elizabeth, 1918, *The Web of Indian Life*, Longmangreen & Co., Bombay.

Nyogi, T.K., 1979, "Universalization of the Local Deity Panchamanda", in *J. Indian Anthropological Society*, Vol. 14, No. 2.

O'Malley, L.S.S., 1934, *India's Society Heritage.*

———, *Popular Hinduism*, Cambridge University Press.

Panikkar, K.M., 1955, *Hindu Society at Cross Roads.*

Pushalkar, A.D., 1951, *Studies in the Epics and Puranas*, Bharatiya Vidyabhavan, Bombay.

Radcliffe-Brown, 1952, *Structure and Function in Primitive Society.*

Radhakrishnan, S., 1931, *The Hindu View of Life*, New York.

Raghavan, V., 1911, *Prayers, Praises and Psalms*, Madras.

Ramaswami Sastri, K.S., 1978, "The Puranas", in *The Cultural*

Heritage of India, (ed. by S.K. Chatterjee), Vol. 5, Calcutta.

Redfield, R., 1956, *Peasant Society and Culture*, Chicago.

Rice, S., 1937, *Hindu Customs and their Origins*.

Roy, S.C., 1934, "Caste, Race and Religion in India", in *Man in India*, Vol. 14.

Sastri, Nilkanta, K.A., 1975, "An Historical Sketch of Saivism", in *The Cultural Heritage of India*, Vol. IV, Ramakrishna Mission Institute of Culture, Calcutta.

Sinha Surajit and B.N. Saraswati, 1978, *Ascetics of Keshi : An Anthropological Exploration*, N.K. Bose Memorial Foundation, Varanasi.

Singh Raghubir and Singh R.N., 1936, *Malwa in transition*, Bombay.

Sen, Kshitimohan, 1936, *Mediaeval Mysticism of India*, Calcutta.

Sumption, J., 1975, *Pilgrimage : An Image of Mediaeval Religion*, London, Faber & Faber.

Tagore, Rabindranath, 1935, *The Philosophy of our People*, Visvabharati, Shantiniketan.

Swami Pavitrananda, 1975, *Pilgrimage and Fairs : Their Bearing on Indian life* (Vol. 4).

Vikram Smriti, 1948, Ed. by Suryanarayan Vyas, Institute of Oriental Studies, Ujjain.

Tod, J., 1920, *Annals and Antiquities of Rajasthan* (Ed. by W. Crooke), Oxford.

Wagh, J., 1947, *Society of Religion*, London.

Weber, Max, 1952, *Essays in Sociology* (translated).

Zimmer, H., 1951, *Philosophies of India*, New York.

Index